Draft

TREATY
ESTABLISHING A

CONSTITUTION
FOR EUROPE

Adopted by consensus by the European Convention
on 13 June and 10 July 2003

SUBMITTED TO THE
PRESIDENT OF THE EUROPEAN COUNCIL
IN ROME

—— *18 July 2003* ——

the european convention

**Europe Direct is a service to help you find answers
to your questions about the European Union**

**New freephone number:
00 800 6 7 8 9 10 11**

A great deal of additional information on the European Union is available on the Internet.
It can be accessed through the Europa server (http://europa.eu.int).

Cataloguing data can be found at the end of this publication.

Luxembourg: Office for Official Publications of the European Communities, 2003

ISBN 92-78-40197-8

PREFACE

to Parts I and II of the draft Treaty establishing a Constitution for Europe submitted to the European Council meeting in Thessaloniki on 20 June 2003.

Noting that the European Union was coming to a turning point in its existence, the European Council which met in Laeken, Belgium, on 14 and 15 December 2001 convened the European Convention on the Future of Europe.

The Convention was asked to draw up proposals on three subjects: how to bring citizens closer to the European design and European Institutions; how to organise politics and the European political area in an enlarged Union; and how to develop the Union into a stabilising factor and a model in the new world order.

The Convention has identified responses to the questions put in the Laeken declaration:

- it proposes a better division of Union and Member State competences;
- it recommends a merger of the Treaties and the attribution of legal personality to the Union;
- it establishes a simplification of the Union's instruments of action;
- it proposes measures to increase the democracy, transparency and efficiency of the European Union, by developing the contribution of national Parliaments to the legitimacy of the European design, by simplifying the decision-making processes, and by making the functioning of the European Institutions more transparent and comprehensible;
- it establishes the necessary measures to improve the structure and enhance the role of each of the Union's three institutions, taking account, in particular, of the consequences of cnlargement.

The Laeken declaration also asked whether the simplification and reorganisation of the Treaties should not pave the way for the adoption of a constitutional text. The Convention's proceedings ultimately led to the drawing up of a draft Treaty establishing a Constitution for Europe, which achieved a broad consensus at the plenary session on 13 June 2003.

That is the text which it is our privilege to present today, 20 June 2003, to the European Council meeting in Thessaloniki, on behalf of the European Convention, in the hope that it will constitute the foundation of a future Treaty establishing the European Constitution.

V. Giscard d'Estaing

Valéry Giscard d'Estaing
Voorzitter

Giuliano Amato

Giuliano Amato
Vice-voorzitter

Dehaene

Jean-Luc Dehaene
Vice-voorzitter

DRAFT

TREATY ESTABLISHING A CONSTITUTION FOR EUROPE

PREAMBLE

Χρώμεθα γὰρ πολιτείᾳ... καὶ ὄνομα μὲν διὰ τὸ μὴ ἐς ὀλίγους ἀλλ᾽ ἐς πλείονας οἰκεῖν δημοκρατία κέκληται.

Our Constitution ... is called a democracy because power is in the hands not of a minority but of the greatest number.

Thucydides II, 37

Conscious that Europe is a continent that has brought forth civilisation; that its inhabitants, arriving in successive waves from earliest times, have gradually developed the values underlying humanism: equality of persons, freedom, respect for reason,

Drawing inspiration from the cultural, religious and humanist inheritance of Europe, the values of which, still present in its heritage, have embedded within the life of society the central role of the human person and his or her inviolable and inalienable rights, and respect for law,

Believing that reunited Europe intends to continue along the path of civilisation, progress and prosperity, for the good of all its inhabitants, including the weakest and most deprived; that it wishes to remain a continent open to culture, learning and social progress; and that it wishes to deepen the democratic and transparent nature of its public life, and to strive for peace, justice and solidarity throughout the world,

Convinced that, while remaining proud of their own national identities and history, the peoples of Europe are determined to transcend their ancient divisions and, united ever more closely, to forge a common destiny,

Convinced that, thus "united in its diversity", Europe offers them the best chance of pursuing, with due regard for the rights of each individual and in awareness of their responsibilities towards future generations and the Earth, the great venture which makes of it a special area of human hope,

Grateful to the members of the European Convention for having prepared this Constitution on behalf of the citizens and States of Europe,

[Who, having exchanged their full powers, found in good and due form, have agreed as follows:]

PART I

DEFINITION AND OBJECTIVES OF THE UNION

Article 1   ESTABLISHMENT OF THE UNION

1.   Reflecting the will of the citizens and States of Europe to build a common future, this Constitution establishes the European Union, on which the Member States confer competences to attain objectives they have in common. The Union shall coordinate the policies by which the Member States aim to achieve these objectives, and shall exercise in the Community way the competences they confer on it.

2.   The Union shall be open to all European States which respect its values and are committed to promoting them together.

Article 2   THE UNION'S VALUES

The Union is founded on the values of respect for human dignity, liberty, democracy, equality, the rule of law and respect for human rights. These values are common to the Member States in a society of pluralism, tolerance, justice, solidarity and non-discrimination.

Article 3   THE UNION'S OBJECTIVES

1.   The Union's aim is to promote peace, its values and the well-being of its peoples.

2.   The Union shall offer its citizens an area of freedom, security and justice without internal frontiers, and a single market where competition is free and undistorted.

3.   The Union shall work for the sustainable development of Europe based on balanced economic growth, a social market economy, highly competitive and aiming at full employment and social progress, and with a high level of protection and improvement of the quality of the environment. It shall promote scientific and technological advance.

It shall combat social exclusion and discrimination, and shall promote social justice and protection, equality between women and men, solidarity between generations and protection of children's rights.

It shall promote economic, social and territorial cohesion, and solidarity among Member States.

The Union shall respect its rich cultural and linguistic diversity, and shall ensure that Europe's cultural heritage is safeguarded and enhanced.

4.   In its relations with the wider world, the Union shall uphold and promote its values and interests. It shall contribute to peace, security, the sustainable development of the earth, solidarity and mutual respect among peoples, free and fair trade, eradication of poverty and protection of human rights and in particular children's rights, as well as to strict observance and development of international law, including respect for the principles of the United Nations Charter.

5.   These objectives shall be pursued by appropriate means, depending on the extent to which the relevant competences are attributed to the Union in the Constitution.

Article 4   FUNDAMENTAL FREEDOMS AND NON-DISCRIMINATION

1.   Free movement of persons, goods, services and capital, and freedom of establishment shall be guaranteed within and by the Union, in accordance with the provisions of the Constitution.

2.   In the field of application of the Constitution, and without prejudice to any of its specific provisions, any discrimination on grounds of nationality shall be prohibited.

Article 5   RELATIONS BETWEEN THE UNION AND THE MEMBER STATES

1.   The Union shall respect the national identities of the Member States, inherent in their fundamental structures, political and constitutional, inclusive of regional and local self-government. It shall respect their essential State functions, including those for

ensuring the territorial integrity of the State, and for maintaining law and order and safe-guarding internal security.

2.   Following the principle of loyal cooperation, the Union and the Member States shall, in full mutual respect, assist each other in carrying out tasks which flow from the Constitution.

The Member States shall facilitate the achievement of the Union's tasks and refrain from any measure which could jeopardise the attainment of the objectives set out in the Constitution.

Article 6   LEGAL PERSONALITY

The Union shall have legal personality.

FUNDAMENTAL RIGHTS AND CITIZENSHIP OF THE UNION

Article 7   FUNDAMENTAL RIGHTS

1.   The Union shall recognise the rights, freedoms and principles set out in the Charter of Fundamental Rights which constitutes Part II of the Constitution.

2.   The Union shall seek accession to the European Convention for the Protection of Human Rights and Fundamental Freedoms. Such accession shall not affect the Union's competences as defined in the Constitution.

3.   Fundamental rights, as guaranteed by the European Convention for the Protection of Human Rights and Fundamental Freedoms, and as they result from the constitutional traditions common to the Member States, shall constitute general principles of the Union's law.

Article 8   CITIZENSHIP OF THE UNION

1.   Every national of a Member State shall be a citizen of the Union. Citizenship of the Union shall be additional to national citizenship; it shall not replace it.

2.   Citizens of the Union shall enjoy the rights and be subject to the duties provided for in the Constitution. They shall have:

- the right to move and reside freely within the territory of the Member States;
- the right to vote and to stand as candidates in elections to the European Parliament and in municipal elections in their Member State of residence, under the same conditions as nationals of that State;
- the right to enjoy, in the territory of a third country in which the Member State of which they are nationals is not represented, the protection of the diplomatic and consular authorities of any Member State on the same conditions as the nationals of that State;
- the right to petition the European Parliament, to apply to the European Ombudsman, and to address the Institutions and advisory bodies of the

Union in any of the Constitution's languages and to obtain a reply in the same language.

3.   These rights shall be exercised in accordance with the conditions and limits defined by the Constitution and by the measures adopted to give it effect.

Title III   UNION COMPETENCES

Article 9   FUNDAMENTAL PRINCIPLES

1.   The limits of Union competences are governed by the principle of conferral. The use of Union competences is governed by the principles of subsidiarity and proportionality.

2.   Under the principle of conferral, the Union shall act within the limits of the competences conferred upon it by the Member States in the Constitution to attain the objectives set out in the Constitution. Competences not conferred upon the Union in the Constitution remain with the Member States.

3.   Under the principle of subsidiarity, in areas which do not fall within its exclusive competence the Union shall act only if and insofar as the objectives of the intended action cannot be sufficiently achieved by the Member States, either at central level or at regional and local level, but can rather, by reason of the scale or effects of the proposed action, be better achieved at Union level.

The Union Institutions shall apply the principle of subsidiarity as laid down in the Protocol on the application of the principles of subsidiarity and proportionality, annexed to the Constitution. National Parliaments shall ensure compliance with that principle in accordance with the procedure set out in the Protocol.

4.   Under the principle of proportionality, the content and form of Union action shall not exceed what is necessary to achieve the objectives of the Constitution.

The Institutions shall apply the principle of proportionality as laid down in the Protocol referred to in paragraph 3.

Article 10   UNION LAW

1.   The Constitution, and law adopted by the Union's Institutions in exercising competences conferred on it, shall have primacy over the law of the Member States.

2.   Member States shall take all appropriate measures, general or particular, to ensure fulfilment of the obligations flowing from the Constitution or resulting from the Union Institutions' acts.

Article 11   CATEGORIES OF COMPETENCE

1.   When the Constitution confers on the Union exclusive competence in a specific area, only the Union may legislate and adopt legally binding acts, the Member States being able to do so themselves only if so empowered by the Union or for the implementation of acts adopted by the Union.

2.   When the Constitution confers on the Union a competence shared with the Member States in a specific area, the Union and the Member States shall have the power to legislate and adopt legally binding acts in that area. The Member States shall exercise their competence to the extent that the Union has not exercised, or has decided to cease exercising, its competence.

3.   The Union shall have competence to promote and coordinate the economic and employment policies of the Member States.

4.   The Union shall have competence to define and implement a common foreign and security policy, including the progressive framing of a common defence policy.

5.   In certain areas and in the conditions laid down in the Constitution, the Union shall have competence to carry out actions to support, coordinate or supplement the actions of the Member States, without thereby superseding their competence in these areas.

6.   The scope of and arrangements for exercising the Union's competences shall be determined by the provisions specific to each area in Part III.

Article 12   EXCLUSIVE COMPETENCE

1.   The Union shall have exclusive competence to establish the competition rules necessary for the functioning of the internal market, and in the following areas:

  – monetary policy, for the Member States which have adopted the euro,
  – common commercial policy,
  – customs union,
  – the conservation of marine biological resources under the common fisheries policy.

2.   The Union shall have exclusive competence for the conclusion of an international agreement when its conclusion is provided for in a legislative act of the Union, is necessary to enable it to exercise its internal competence, or affects an internal Union act.

Article 13   AREAS OF SHARED COMPETENCE

1.   The Union shall share competence with the Member States where the Constitution confers on it a competence which does not relate to the areas referred to in Articles 12 and 16.

2.   Shared competence applies in the following principal areas:

  – internal market,
  – area of freedom, security and justice,
  – agriculture and fisheries, excluding the conservation of marine biological resources,
  – transport and trans-European networks,
  – energy,
  – social policy, for aspects defined in Part III,
  – economic, social and territorial cohesion,
  – environment,
  – consumer protection,
  – common safety concerns in public health matters.

3.   In the areas of research, technological development and space, the Union shall have competence to carry out actions, in particular to define and implement programmes; however, the exercise of that competence may not result in Member States being prevented from exercising theirs.

4.   In the areas of development cooperation and humanitarian aid, the Union shall have competence to take action and conduct a common policy; however, the exercise of that competence may not result in Member States being prevented from exercising theirs.

Article 14   THE COORDINATION OF ECONOMIC AND EMPLOYMENT POLICIES

1.   The Union shall adopt measures to ensure coordination of the economic policies of the Member States, in particular by adopting broad guidelines for these policies. The Member States shall coordinate their economic policies within the Union.

2.   Specific provisions shall apply to those Member States which have adopted the euro.

3.   The Union shall adopt measures to ensure coordination of the employment policies of the Member States, in particular by adopting guidelines for these policies.

4.   The Union may adopt initiatives to ensure coordination of Member States' social policies.

Article 15   THE COMMON FOREIGN AND SECURITY POLICY

1.   The Union's competence in matters of common foreign and security policy shall cover all areas of foreign policy and all questions relating to the Union's security, including the progressive framing of a common defence policy, which might lead to a common defence.

2.   Member States shall actively and unreservedly support the Union's common foreign and security policy in a spirit of loyalty and mutual solidarity and shall comply with the acts adopted by the Union in this area. They shall refrain from action contrary to the Union's interests or likely to impair its effectiveness.

Article 16 AREAS OF SUPPORTING, COORDINATING OR
COMPLEMENTARY ACTION

1. The Union may take supporting, coordinating or complementary action.

2. The areas for supporting, coordinating or complementary action shall be, at European level:

  - industry,
  - protection and improvement of human health,
  - education, vocational training, youth and sport,
  - culture,
  - civil protection.

3. Legally binding acts adopted by the Union on the basis of the provisions specific to these areas in Part III may not entail harmonisation of Member States' laws or regulations.

Article 17 FLEXIBILITY CLAUSE

1. If action by the Union should prove necessary within the framework of the policies defined in Part III to attain one of the objectives set by the Constitution, and the Constitution has not provided the necessary powers, the Council of Ministers, acting unanimously on a proposal from the Commission and after obtaining the consent of the European Parliament, shall take the appropriate measures.

2. Using the procedure for monitoring the subsidiarity principle referred to in Article 9(3), the Commission shall draw Member States' national Parliaments' attention to proposals based on this Article.

3. Provisions adopted on the basis of this Article may not entail harmonisation of Member States' laws or regulations in cases where the Constitution excludes such harmonisation.

THE UNION'S INSTITUTIONS

THE INSTITUTIONAL FRAMEWORK

Article 18   THE UNION'S INSTITUTIONS

1.   The Union shall be served by a single institutional framework which shall aim to:

- advance the objectives of the Union,
- promote the values of the Union,
- serve the interests of the Union, its citizens and its Member States,

and ensure the consistency, effectiveness and continuity of the policies and actions which it undertakes in pursuit of its objectives.

2.   This institutional framework comprises:

The European Parliament,
The European Council,
The Council of Ministers,
The European Commission,
The Court of Justice.

3.   Each Institution shall act within the limits of the powers conferred on it in the Constitution, and in conformity with the procedures and conditions set out in it. The Institutions shall practice full mutual cooperation.

Article 19   THE EUROPEAN PARLIAMENT

1.   The European Parliament shall, jointly with the Council of Ministers, enact legislation, and exercise the budgetary function, as well as functions of political control and consultation as laid down in the Constitution. It shall elect the President of the European Commission.

2.   The European Parliament shall be elected by direct universal suffrage of European citizens in free and secret ballot for a term of five years. Its members shall not exceed seven hundred and thirty-six in number. Representation of European citizens shall be degressively proportional, with a minimum threshold of four members per Member State.

Sufficiently in advance of the European Parliamentary elections in 2009, and, as necessary thereafter for further elections, the European Council shall adopt by unanimity, on the basis of a proposal from the European Parliament and with its consent, a decision establishing the composition of the European Parliament, respecting the principles set out above.

3.   The European Parliament shall elect its President and its officers from among its members.

Article 20   THE EUROPEAN COUNCIL

1.   The European Council shall provide the Union with the necessary impetus for its development, and shall define its general political directions and priorities. It does not exercise legislative functions.

2.   The European Council shall consist of the Heads of State or Government of the Member States, together with its President and the President of the Commission. The Union Minister for Foreign Affairs shall take part in its work.

3.   The European Council shall meet quarterly, convened by its President. When the agenda so requires, its members may decide to be assisted by a minister and, in the case of the President of the Commission, a European Commissioner. When the situation so requires, the President shall convene a special meeting of the European Council.

4.   Except where the Constitution provides otherwise, decisions of the European Council shall be taken by consensus.

Article 21   THE EUROPEAN COUNCIL CHAIR

1.   The European Council shall elect its President, by qualified majority, for a term of two and a half years, renewable once. In the event of an impediment or serious misconduct, the European Council can end his or her mandate according to the same procedure.

2.   The President of the European Council:

- shall chair it and drive forward its work,
- shall ensure its proper preparation and continuity in cooperation with the President of the Commission, and on the basis of the work of the General Affairs Council,
- shall endeavour to facilitate cohesion and consensus within the European Council,
- shall present a report to the European Parliament after each of its meetings.

The President of the European Council shall at his or her level and in that capacity ensure the external representation of the Union on issues concerning its common foreign and security policy, without prejudice to the responsibilities of the Union Minister for Foreign Affairs.

3.   The President of the European Council may not hold a national mandate.

Article 22   THE COUNCIL OF MINISTERS

1.   The Council of Ministers shall, jointly with the European Parliament, enact legislation, exercise the budgetary function and carry out policy-making and coordinating functions, as laid down in the Constitution.

2.   The Council of Ministers shall consist of a representative of each Member State at ministerial level for each of its formations. Only this representative may commit the Member State in question and cast its vote.

3.   Except where the Constitution provides otherwise, decisions of the Council of Ministers shall be taken by qualified majority.

Article 23   FORMATIONS OF THE COUNCIL OF MINISTERS

1.   The Legislative and General Affairs Council shall ensure consistency in the work of the Council of Ministers.

When it acts in its General Affairs function, it shall, in liaison with the Commission, prepare, and ensure follow-up to, meetings of the European Council.

When it acts in its legislative function, the Council of Ministers shall consider and, jointly with the European Parliament, enact European laws and European framework laws, in accordance with the provisions of the Constitution. In this function, each Member State's representation shall include one or two representatives at ministerial level with relevant expertise, reflecting the business on the agenda of the Council of Ministers.

2.   The Foreign Affairs Council shall, on the basis of strategic guidelines laid down by the European Council, flesh out the Union's external policies, and ensure that its actions are consistent. It shall be chaired by the Union Minister for Foreign Affairs.

3.   The European Council shall adopt a European decision establishing further formations in which the Council of Ministers may meet.

4.   The Presidency of Council of Ministers formations, other than that of Foreign Affairs, shall be held by Member State representatives within the Council of Ministers on the basis of equal rotation for periods of at least a year. The European Council shall adopt a European decision establishing the rules of such rotation, taking into account European political and geographical balance and the diversity of Member States.

Article 24   QUALIFIED MAJORITY

1.   When the European Council or the Council of Ministers takes decisions by qualified majority, such a majority shall consist of the majority of Member States, representing at least three fifths of the population of the Union.

2.   When the Constitution does not require the European Council or the Council of Ministers to act on the basis of a proposal of the Commission, or when the European Council or the Council of Ministers is not acting on the initiative of the Union

Minister for Foreign Affairs, the required qualified majority shall consist of two thirds of the Member States, representing at least three fifths of the population of the Union.

3.   The provisions of paragraphs 1 and 2 shall take effect on 1 November 2009, after the European Parliament elections have taken place, according to the provisions of Article 19.

4.   Where the Constitution provides in Part III for European laws and frame-work laws to be adopted by the Council of Ministers according to a special legislative procedure, the European Council can adopt, on its own initiative and by unanimity, after a period of consideration of at least six months, a decision allowing for the adoption of such European laws or framework laws according to the ordinary legislative procedure. The European Council shall act after consulting the European Parliament and informing the national Parliaments.

Where the Constitution provides in Part III for the Council of Ministers to act unanimously in a given area, the European Council can adopt, on its own initiative and by unanimity, a European decision allowing the Council of Ministers to act by qualified majority in that area. Any initiative taken by the European Council under this subparagraph shall be sent to national Parliaments no less than four months before any decision is taken on it.

5.   Within the European Council, its President and the President of the Commission do not vote.

Article 25   THE EUROPEAN COMMISSION

1.   The European Commission shall promote the general European interest and take appropriate initiatives to that end. It shall ensure the application of the Constitution, and steps taken by the Institutions under the Constitution. It shall oversee the application of Union law under the control of the Court of Justice. It shall execute the budget and manage programmes. It shall exercise coordinating, executive and management functions, as laid down in the Constitution. With the exception of the common foreign and security policy, and other cases provided for in the Constitution, it shall ensure the Union's external representation. It shall initiate the Union's annual and multiannual programming with a view to achieving interinstitutional agreements.

2. Except where the Constitution provides otherwise, Union legislative acts can be adopted only on the basis of a Commission proposal. Other acts are adopted on the basis of a Commission proposal where the Constitution so provides.

3. The Commission shall consist of a College comprising its President, the Union Minister for Foreign Affairs/Vice-President, and thirteen European Commissioners selected on the basis of a system of equal rotation between the Member States. This system shall be established by a European decision adopted by the European Council on the basis of the following principles:

(a) Member States shall be treated on a strictly equal footing as regards determination of the sequence of, and the time spent by, their nationals as Members of the College; consequently, the difference between the total number of terms of office held by nationals of any given pair of Member States may never be more than one;

(b) subject to point (a), each successive College shall be so composed as to reflect satisfactorily the demographic and geographical range of all the Member States of the Union.

The Commission President shall appoint non-voting Commissioners, chosen according to the same criteria as apply for Members of the College and coming from all other Member States.

These arrangements shall take effect on 1 November 2009.

4. In carrying out its responsibilities, the Commission shall be completely independent. In the discharge of their duties, the European Commissioners and Commissioners shall neither seek nor take instructions from any government or other body.

5. The Commission, as a College, shall be responsible to the European Parliament. The Commission President shall be responsible to the European Parliament for the activities of the Commissioners. Under the procedures set out in Article III-243, the European Parliament may pass a censure motion on the Commission. If such a motion is passed, the European Commissioners and Commissioners must all resign. The Commission shall continue to handle everyday business until a new College is nominated.

Article 26   THE PRESIDENT OF THE EUROPEAN COMMISSION

1.   Taking into account the elections to the European Parliament and after appropriate consultations, the European Council, deciding by qualified majority, shall put to the European Parliament its proposed candidate for the Presidency of the Commission. This candidate shall be elected by the European Parliament by a majority of its members. If this candidate does not receive the required majority support, the European Council shall within one month propose a new candidate to the European Parliament, following the same procedure.

2.   Each Member State determined by the system of rotation shall establish a list of three persons, in which both genders shall be represented, whom it considers qualified to be a European Commissioner. By choosing one person from each of the proposed lists, the President-elect shall select the thirteen European Commissioners for their competence, European commitment, and guaranteed independence. The President and the persons so nominated for membership of the College, including the future Union Minister for Foreign Affairs, as well as the persons nominated as non-voting Commissioners, shall be submitted collectively to a vote of approval by the European Parliament. The Commission's term of office shall be five years.

3.   The President of the Commission shall:

- lay down guidelines within which the Commission is to work;
- decide its internal organisation, ensuring that it acts consistently, efficiently and on a collegiate basis;
- appoint Vice-Presidents from among the members of the College.

A European Commissioner or Commissioner shall resign if the President so requests.

Article 27   THE UNION MINISTER FOR FOREIGN AFFAIRS

1.   The European Council, acting by qualified majority, with the agreement of the President of the Commission, shall appoint the Union Minister for Foreign Affairs. He or she shall conduct the Union's common foreign and security policy. The European Council may end his or her tenure by the same procedure.

2.　　　　　The Union Minister for Foreign Affairs shall contribute by his or her proposals to the development of the common foreign policy, which he or she shall carry out
as mandated by the Council of Ministers. The same shall apply to the common security
and defence policy.

3.　　　　　The Union Minister for Foreign Affairs shall be one of the Vice-Presidents
of the Commission. He or she shall be responsible there for handling external relations
and for coordinating other aspects of the Union's external action. In exercising these
responsibilities within the Commission, and only for these responsibilities, the Union
Minister for Foreign Affairs shall be bound by Commission procedures.

Article 28　　THE COURT OF JUSTICE

1.　　　　　The Court of Justice shall include the European Court of Justice, the High
Court and specialised courts. It shall ensure respect for the law in the interpretation and
application of the Constitution.

Member States shall provide rights of appeal sufficient to ensure effective legal protection
in the field of Union law.

2.　　　　　The European Court of Justice shall consist of one judge from each
Member State, and shall be assisted by Advocates-General.

The High Court shall include at least one judge per Member State: the number shall be
fixed by the Statute of the Court of Justice.

The judges and the Advocates-General of the European Court of Justice and the judges
of the High Court, chosen from persons whose independence is beyond doubt and who
satisfy the conditions set out in Articles III-260 and III-261, shall be appointed by common accord of the governments of the Member States for a term of six years, renewable.

3.　　　　　The Court of Justice shall:

- rule on actions brought by a Member State, an Institution or a natural
  or legal person in accordance with the provisions of Part III;
- give preliminary rulings, at the request of Member State courts, on the
  interpretation of Union law or the validity of acts adopted by the
  Institutions;
- rule on the other cases provided for in the Constitution.

Chapter II OTHER INSTITUTIONS AND BODIES

Article 29 THE EUROPEAN CENTRAL BANK

1.　　　The European Central Bank, together with the national central banks, shall constitute the European System of Central Banks. The European Central Bank, together with the national central banks of the Member States which have adopted the Union currency, the euro, shall conduct the monetary policy of the Union.

2.　　　The European System of Central Banks shall be governed by the decision-making bodies of the European Central Bank. The primary objective of the European System of Central Banks shall be to maintain price stability. Without prejudice to the objective of price stability, it shall support general economic policies in the Union with a view to contributing to the achievement of the Union's objectives. It shall conduct other Central Bank tasks according to the provisions of Part III and the Statute of the European System of Central Banks and the European Central Bank.

3.　　　The European Central Bank is an Institution which has legal personality. It alone may authorise the issue of the euro. In the exercise of its powers and for its finances, it shall be independent. Union Institutions and bodies, and the governments of the Member States, shall undertake to respect this principle.

4.　　　The European Central Bank shall adopt such measures as are necessary to carry out its tasks in accordance with the provisions of Articles III-77 to III-83 and Article III-90, and with the conditions laid down in the Statute of the European System of Central Banks and the European Central Bank. In accordance with these same provisions, those Member States which have not adopted the euro, and their central banks, shall retain their powers in monetary matters.

5.　　　Within its areas of competence, the European Central Bank shall be consulted on all proposed Union acts, and all proposals for regulation at national level, and may give an opinion.

6.　　　The decision-making organs of the European Central Bank, their composition and operating methods are set out in Articles III-84 to III-87, as well as in the Statute of the European System of Central Banks and of the European Central Bank.

Article 30   THE COURT OF AUDITORS

1.   The Court of Auditors is the Institution which shall carry out the audit.

2.   It shall examine the accounts of all Union revenue and expenditure, and shall ensure good financial management.

3.   It shall consist of one national of each Member State. In the performance of their duties, its members shall be completely independent.

Article 31   THE UNION'S ADVISORY BODIES

1.   The European Parliament, the Council of Ministers and the Commission shall be assisted by a Committee of the Regions and an Economic and Social Committee, exercising advisory functions.

2.   The Committee of the Regions shall consist of representatives of regional and local bodies who either hold a regional or local authority electoral mandate or are politically accountable to an elected assembly.

3.   The Economic and Social Committee shall consist of representatives of organisations of employers, of the employed, and of others representative of civil society, notably in socio-economic, civic, professional and cultural areas.

4.   The members of the Committee of the Regions and the Economic and Social Committee must not be bound by any mandatory instructions. They shall be completely independent, in the performance of their duties, in the Union's general interest.

5.   Rules governing the composition of these Committees, the designation of their members, their powers and their operations, are set out in Articles III-292 to III-298. The rules governing their composition shall be reviewed at regular intervals by the Council of Ministers, on the basis of a Commission proposal, in the light of economic, social and demographic developments within the Union.

EXERCISE OF UNION COMPETENCE

COMMON PROVISIONS

Article 32   ### THE LEGAL ACTS OF THE UNION

1.   In exercising the competences conferred on it in the Constitution, the Union shall use as legal instruments, in accordance with the provisions of Part III, European laws, European framework laws, European regulations, European decisions, recommendations and opinions.

A European law shall be a legislative act of general application. It shall be binding in its entirety and directly applicable in all Member States.

A European framework law shall be a legislative act binding, as to the result to be achieved, on the Member States to which it is addressed, but leaving the national authorities entirely free to choose the form and means of achieving that result.

A European regulation shall be a non-legislative act of general application for the implementation of legislative acts and of certain specific provisions of the Constitution. It may either be binding in its entirety and directly applicable in all Member States, or be binding, as regards the result to be achieved, on all Member States to which it is addressed, but leaving the national authorities entirely free to choose the form and means of achieving that result.

A European decision shall be a non-legislative act, binding in its entirety. A decision which specifies those to whom it is addressed shall be binding only on them.

Recommendations and opinions adopted by the Institutions shall have no binding force.

2.   When considering proposals for legislative acts, the European Parliament and the Council of Ministers shall refrain from adopting acts not provided for by this Article in the area in question.

Article 33   LEGISLATIVE ACTS

1.   European laws and European framework laws shall be adopted, on the basis of proposals from the Commission, jointly by the European Parliament and the Council of Ministers under the ordinary legislative procedure as set out in Article III-302. If the two Institutions cannot reach agreement on an act, it shall not be adopted.

In the cases specifically provided for in Article III-165, European laws and European framework laws may be adopted at the initiative of a group of Member States in accordance with Article III-302.

2.   In the specific cases provided for by the Constitution, European laws and European framework laws shall be adopted by the European Parliament with the participation of the Council of Ministers, or by the latter with the participation of the European Parliament, in accordance with special legislative procedures.

Article 34   NON-LEGISLATIVE ACTS

1.   The Council of Ministers and the Commission shall adopt European regulations or European decisions in the cases referred to in Articles 35 and 36 and in the cases specifically provided for in the Constitution. The European Council shall adopt European decisions in the cases specifically provided for in the Constitution. The European Central Bank shall adopt European regulations and European decisions when authorised to do so by the Constitution.

2.   The Council of Ministers and the Commission, and the European Central Bank when so authorised in the Constitution, adopt recommendations.

Article 35   DELEGATED REGULATIONS

1.   European laws and European framework laws may delegate to the Commission the power to enact delegated regulations to supplement or amend certain non-essential elements of the European law or framework law.

The objectives, content, scope and duration of the delegation shall be explicitly defined in the European laws and framework laws. A delegation may not cover the essential elements of an area. These shall be reserved for the European law or framework law.

2.   The conditions of application to which the delegation is subject shall be explicitly determined in the European laws and framework laws. They may consist of the following possibilities:

- the European Parliament or the Council of Ministers may decide to revoke the delegation;
- the delegated regulation may enter into force only if no objection has been expressed by the European Parliament or the Council of Ministers within a period set by the European law or framework law.

For the purposes of the preceding paragraph, the European Parliament shall act by a majority of its members, and the Council of Ministers by a qualified majority.

Article 36   IMPLEMENTING ACTS

1.   Member States shall adopt all measures of national law necessary to implement legally binding Union acts.

2.   Where uniform conditions for implementing binding Union acts are needed, those acts may confer implementing powers on the Commission, or, in specific cases duly justified and in the cases provided for in Article 39, on the Council of Ministers.

3.   The European laws shall lay down in advance rules and general principles for the mechanisms for control by Member States of Union implementing acts.

4.   Union implementing acts shall take the form of European implementing regulations or European implementing decisions.

Article 37   PRINCIPLES COMMON TO THE UNION'S LEGAL ACTS

1.   Unless the Constitution contains a specific stipulation, the Institutions shall decide, in compliance with the procedures applicable, the type of act to be adopted in each case, in accordance with the principle of proportionality set out in Article 9.

2.   European laws, European framework laws, European regulations and European decisions shall state the reasons on which they are based and shall refer to any proposals or opinions required by the Constitution.

Article 38   PUBLICATION AND ENTRY INTO FORCE

1.   European laws and framework laws adopted under the ordinary legislative procedure shall be signed by the President of the European Parliament and by the President of the Council of Ministers. In other cases they shall be signed by the President of the European Parliament or by the President of the Council of Ministers. European laws and European framework laws shall be published in the Official Journal of the European Union and shall enter into force on the date specified in them or, in the absence of such a stated date, on the twentieth day following their publication.

2.   European regulations and European decisions which do not specify to whom they are addressed or which are addressed to all Member States shall be signed by the President of the Institution which adopts them, shall be published in the Official Journal of the European Union and shall enter into force on the date specified in them or, in the absence of such a stated date, on the twentieth day following their publication.

3.   Other decisions shall be notified to those to whom they are addressed and shall take effect upon such notification.

Chapter II   SPECIFIC PROVISIONS

Article 39   SPECIFIC PROVISIONS FOR IMPLEMENTING COMMON
FOREIGN AND SECURITY POLICY

1.   The European Union shall conduct a common foreign and security policy, based on the development of mutual political solidarity among Member States, the identification of questions of general interest and the achievement of an ever-increasing degree of convergence of Member States' actions.

2.   The European Council shall identify the Union's strategic interests and determine the objectives of its common foreign and security policy. The Council of Ministers shall frame this policy within the framework of the strategic guidelines established by the European Council and in accordance with the arrangements in Part III.

3.   The European Council and the Council of Ministers shall adopt the necessary European decisions.

4.   The common foreign and security policy shall be put into effect by the Union Minister for Foreign Affairs and by the Member States, using national and Union resources.

5.   Member States shall consult one another within the European Council and the Council of Ministers on any foreign and security policy issue which is of general interest in order to determine a common approach. Before undertaking any action on the international scene or any commitment which could affect the Union's interests, each Member State shall consult the others within the European Council or the Council of Ministers. Member States shall ensure, through the convergence of their actions, that the Union is able to assert its interests and values on the international scene. Member States shall show mutual solidarity.

6.   The European Parliament shall be regularly consulted on the main aspects and basic choices of the common foreign and security policy and shall be kept informed of how it evolves.

7.   European decisions relating to the common foreign and security policy shall be adopted by the European Council and the Council of Ministers unanimously, except

in the cases referred to in Part III. The European Council and the Council of Ministers shall act on a proposal from a Member State, from the Union Minister for Foreign Affairs or from that Minister with the Commission's support. European laws and European framework laws are excluded.

8.   The European Council may unanimously decide that the Council of Ministers should act by qualified majority in cases other than those referred to in Part III.

Article 40   SPECIFIC PROVISIONS FOR IMPLEMENTING THE
              COMMON SECURITY AND DEFENCE POLICY

1.   The common security and defence policy shall be an integral part of the common foreign and security policy. It shall provide the Union with an operational capacity drawing on assets civil and military. The Union may use them on missions outside the Union for peace-keeping, conflict prevention and strengthening international security in accordance with the principles of the United Nations Charter. The performance of these tasks shall be undertaken using capabilities provided by the Member States.

2.   The common security and defence policy shall include the progressive framing of a common Union defence policy. This will lead to a common defence, when the European Council, acting unanimously, so decides. It shall in that case recommend to the Member States the adoption of such a decision in accordance with their respective constitutional requirements.

The policy of the Union in accordance with this Article shall not prejudice the specific character of the security and defence policy of certain Member States and shall respect the obligations of certain Member States, which see their common defence realised in the North Atlantic Treaty Organisation, under the North Atlantic Treaty, and be compatible with the common security and defence policy established within that framework.

3.   Member States shall make civilian and military capabilities available to the Union for the implementation of the common security and defence policy, to contribute to the objectives defined by the Council of Ministers. Those Member States which together establish multinational forces may also make them available to the common security and defence policy.

Member States shall undertake progressively to improve their military capabilities. A European Armaments, Research and Military Capabilities Agency shall be established to identify operational requirements, to promote measures to satisfy those requirements, to contribute to identifying and, where appropriate, implementing any measure needed to strengthen the industrial and technological base of the defence sector, to participate in defining a European capabilities and armaments policy, and to assist the Council of Ministers in evaluating the improvement of military capabilities.

4.   European decisions on the implementation of the common security and defence policy, including those initiating a mission as referred to in this Article, shall be adopted by the Council of Ministers acting unanimously on a proposal from the Union Minister for Foreign Affairs or from a Member State. The Union Minister for Foreign Affairs may propose the use of both national resources and Union instruments, together with the Commission where appropriate.

5.   The Council of Ministers may entrust the execution of a task, within the Union framework, to a group of Member States in order to protect the Union's values and serve its interests. The execution of such a task shall be governed by Article III-211.

6.   Those Member States whose military capabilities fulfil higher criteria and which have made more binding commitments to one another in this area with a view to the most demanding missions shall establish structured cooperation within the Union framework. Such cooperation shall be governed by the provisions of Article III-213.

7.   Until such time as the European Council has acted in accordance with paragraph 2 of this Article, closer cooperation shall be established, in the Union framework, as regards mutual defence. Under this cooperation, if one of the Member States participating in such cooperation is the victim of armed aggression on its territory, the other participating States shall give it aid and assistance by all the means in their power, military or other, in accordance with Article 51 of the United Nations Charter. In the execution of closer cooperation on mutual defence, the participating Member States shall work in close cooperation with the North Atlantic Treaty Organisation. The detailed arrangements for participation in this cooperation and its operation, and the relevant decision-making procedures, are set out in Article III-214.

8.   The European Parliament shall be regularly consulted on the main aspects and basic choices of the common security and defence policy, and shall be kept informed of how it evolves.

Article 41   SPECIFIC PROVISIONS FOR IMPLEMENTING THE AREA OF
FREEDOM, SECURITY AND JUSTICE

1.   The Union shall constitute an area of freedom, security and justice:

– by adopting European laws and framework laws intended, where necessary, to approximate national laws in the areas listed in Part III;
– by promoting mutual confidence between the competent authorities of
the Member States, in particular on the basis of mutual recognition of
judicial and extrajudicial decisions;
– by operational cooperation between the competent authorities of the
Member States, including the police, customs and other services special-
ising in the prevention and detection of criminal offences.

2.   Within the area of freedom, security and justice, national parliaments may
participate in the evaluation mechanisms foreseen in Article III-161, and shall be
involved in the political monitoring of Europol and the evaluation of Eurojust's activities
in accordance with Articles III-177 and III-174.

3.   In the field of police and judicial cooperation in criminal matters, Member
States shall have a right of initiative in accordance with Article III-160 of the
Constitution.

Article 42   SOLIDARITY CLAUSE

1.   The Union and its Member States shall act jointly in a spirit of solidarity if
a Member State is the victim of terrorist attack or natural or man-made disaster. The
Union shall mobilise all the instruments at its disposal, including the military resources
made available by the Member States, to:

(a) – prevent the terrorist threat in the territory of the Member States;
– protect democratic institutions and the civilian population from any
terrorist attack;
– assist a Member State in its territory at the request of its political
authorities in the event of a terrorist attack;

(b) – assist a Member State in its territory at the request of its political authorities in the event of a disaster.

2. The detailed arrangements for implementing this provision are at Article III-231.

Chapter III

ENHANCED COOPERATION

Article 43   ENHANCED COOPERATION

1.   Member States which wish to establish enhanced cooperation between themselves within the framework of the Union's non-exclusive competences may make use of its Institutions and exercise those competences by applying the relevant provisions of the Constitution, subject to the limits and in accordance with the procedures laid down in this Article and in Articles III-322 to III-329.

Enhanced cooperation shall aim to further the objectives of the Union, protect its interests and reinforce its integration process. Such cooperation shall be open to all Member States when it is being established and at any time, in accordance with Article III-324.

2.   Authorisation to proceed with enhanced cooperation shall be granted by the Council of Ministers as a last resort, when it has been established within the Council of Ministers that the objectives of such cooperation cannot be attained within a reasonable period by the Union as a whole, and provided that it brings together at least one third of the Member States. The Council of Ministers shall act in accordance with the procedure laid down in Article III-325.

3.   Only members of the Council of Ministers representing the States participating in enhanced cooperation shall take part in the adoption of acts. All Member States may, however, take part in the deliberations of the Council of Ministers.

Unanimity shall be constituted by the votes of the representatives of the participating States only. A qualified majority shall be defined as a majority of the votes of the representatives of the participating States, representing at least three fifths of the population of those States. Where the Constitution does not require the Council of Ministers to act on the basis of a Commission proposal, or where the Council of Ministers is not acting upon initiative of the Minister for Foreign Affairs, the required qualified majority shall be defined as a majority of two thirds of the participating States, representing at least three fifths of the population of those States.

4.   Acts adopted in the framework of enhanced cooperation shall bind only participating States. They shall not be regarded as an acquis which has to be accepted by candidates for accession to the Union.

Title VI   THE DEMOCRATIC LIFE OF THE UNION

Article 44   THE PRINCIPLE OF DEMOCRATIC EQUALITY

In all its activities, the Union shall observe the principle of the equality of citizens. All shall receive equal attention from the Union's Institutions.

Article 45   THE PRINCIPLE OF REPRESENTATIVE DEMOCRACY

1.   The working of the Union shall be founded on the principle of representative democracy.

2.   Citizens are directly represented at Union level in the European Parliament. Member States are represented in the European Council and in the Council of Ministers by their governments, themselves accountable to national parliaments, elected by their citizens.

3.   Every citizen shall have the right to participate in the democratic life of the Union. Decisions shall be taken as openly as possible and as closely as possible to the citizen.

4.   Political parties at European level contribute to forming European political awareness and to expressing the will of Union citizens.

Article 46   THE PRINCIPLE OF PARTICIPATORY DEMOCRACY

1.   The Union Institutions shall, by appropriate means, give citizens and representative associations the opportunity to make known and publicly exchange their views in all areas of Union action.

2.   The Union Institutions shall maintain an open, transparent and regular dialogue with representative associations and civil society.

3.   The Commission shall carry out broad consultations with parties concerned in order to ensure that the Union's actions are coherent and transparent.

4.   No less than one million citizens coming from a significant number of Member States may invite the Commission to submit any appropriate proposal on matters where citizens consider that a legal act of the Union is required for the purpose of implementing the Constitution. A European law shall determine the provisions for the specific procedures and conditions required for such a citizens' initiative.

Article 47   THE SOCIAL PARTNERS AND AUTONOMOUS SOCIAL DIALOGUE

The European Union recognises and promotes the role of the social partners at Union level, taking into account the diversity of national systems; it shall facilitate dialogue between the social partners, respecting their autonomy.

Article 48   THE EUROPEAN OMBUDSMAN

A European Ombudsman appointed by the European Parliament shall receive, investigate and report on complaints about maladministration within the Union Institutions, bodies or agencies. The European Ombudsman shall be completely independent in the performance of his or her duties.

Article 49   TRANSPARENCY OF THE PROCEEDINGS OF UNION INSTITUTIONS

1.   In order to promote good governance and ensure the participation of civil society, the Union Institutions, bodies and agencies shall conduct their work as openly as possible.

2.   The European Parliament shall meet in public, as shall the Council of Ministers when examining and adopting a legislative proposal.

3.   Any citizen of the Union, and any natural or legal person residing or having its registered office in a Member State shall have a right of access to documents of the

Union Institutions, bodies and agencies in whatever form they are produced, in accordance with the conditions laid down in Part III.

4.   A European law shall lay down the general principles and limits which, on grounds of public or private interest, govern the right of access to such documents.

5.   Each Institution, body or agency referred to in paragraph 3 shall determine in its own rules of procedure specific provisions regarding access to its documents, in accordance with the European law referred to in paragraph 4.

Article 50   PROTECTION OF PERSONAL DATA

1.   Everyone has the right to the protection of personal data concerning him or her.

2.   A European law shall lay down the rules relating to the protection of individuals with regard to the processing of personal data by Union Institutions, bodies and agencies, and by the Member States when carrying out activities which come under the scope of Union law, and the rules relating to the free movement of such data. Compliance with these rules shall be subject to the control of an independent authority.

Article 51   STATUS OF CHURCHES AND NON-CONFESSIONAL
          ORGANISATIONS

1.   The Union respects and does not prejudice the status under national law of churches and religious associations or communities in the Member States.

2.   The Union equally respects the status of philosophical and non-confessional organisations.

3.   Recognising their identity and their specific contribution, the Union shall maintain an open, transparent and regular dialogue with these churches and organisations.

THE UNION'S FINANCES

Article 52 BUDGETARY AND FINANCIAL PRINCIPLES

1. All items of Union revenue and expenditure shall be included in estimates drawn up for each financial year and shall be shown in the budget, in accordance with the provisions of Part III.

2. The revenue and expenditure shown in the budget shall be in balance.

3. The expenditure shown in the budget shall be authorised for the annual budgetary period in accordance with the European law referred to in Article III-318.

4. The implementation of expenditure shown in the budget shall require the prior adoption of a binding legal act providing a legal basis for Union action and for the implementation of the expenditure in accordance with the European law referred to in Article III-318. This act must take the form of a European law, a European framework law, a European regulation or a European decision.

5. With a view to maintaining budgetary discipline, the Union shall not adopt any act which is likely to have appreciable implications for the budget without providing an assurance that the proposal or measure in question is capable of being financed within the limit of the Union's own resources and the multiannual financial framework referred to in Article 54.

6. The Union's budget shall be implemented in accordance with the principle of sound financial management. Member States shall cooperate with the Union to ensure that the appropriations entered in the budget are used in accordance with the principles of sound financial management.

7. The Union and the Member States shall counter fraud and any other illegal activities affecting the financial interests of the Union in accordance with the provisions of Article III-321.

Article 53   THE UNION'S RESOURCES

1.   The Union shall provide itself with the means necessary to attain its objectives and carry through its policies.

2.   Without prejudice to other revenue, the Union's budget shall be financed wholly from its own resources.

3.   A European law of the Council of Ministers shall lay down the limit of the Union's resources and may establish new categories of resources or abolish an existing category. That law shall not enter into force until it is approved by the Member States in accordance with their respective constitutional requirements. The Council of Ministers shall act unanimously after consulting the European Parliament.

4.   A European law of the Council shall lay down the modalities relating to the Union's resources. The Council of Ministers shall act after obtaining the consent of the European Parliament.

Article 54   THE MULTIANNUAL FINANCIAL FRAMEWORK

1.   The multiannual financial framework shall ensure that Union expenditure develops in an orderly manner and within the own resources limits. It shall determine the amounts of the annual ceilings for commitment appropriations by category of expenditure in accordance with the provisions of Article III-308.

2.   A European law of the Council of Ministers shall lay down the multiannual financial framework. The Council of Ministers shall act after obtaining the consent of the European Parliament, which shall be given by a majority of its component members.

3.   The annual budget of the Union shall comply with the multiannual financial framework.

4.   The Council of Ministers shall act unanimously when adopting the first multiannual financial framework following the entry into force of the Constitution.

Article 55   THE UNION'S BUDGET

The European Parliament and the Council of Ministers shall, on a proposal from the Commission and in accordance with the arrangements laid down in Article III-310, adopt the European law determining the Union's annual budget.

Title VIII — THE UNION AND ITS IMMEDIATE ENVIRONMENT

Article 56 — THE UNION AND ITS IMMEDIATE ENVIRONMENT

1.　　　　The Union shall develop a special relationship with neighbouring States, aiming to establish an area of prosperity and good neighbourliness, founded on the values of the Union and characterised by close and peaceful relations based on cooperation.

2.　　　　For this purpose, the Union may conclude and implement specific agreements with the countries concerned in accordance with Article III-227. These agreements may contain reciprocal rights and obligations as well as the possibility of undertaking activities jointly. Their implementation shall be the subject of periodic consultation.

UNION MEMBERSHIP

Article 57 CONDITIONS OF ELIGIBILITY
AND PROCEDURE FOR ACCESSION TO THE UNION

1. The Union shall be open to all European States which respect the values referred to in Article 2, and are committed to promoting them together.

2. Any European State which wishes to become a member of the Union shall address its application to the Council of Ministers. The European Parliament and the Member States' national Parliaments shall be notified of this application. The Council of Ministers shall act unanimously after consulting the Commission and after obtaining the consent of the European Parliament. The conditions and arrangements for admission shall be the subject of an agreement between the Member States and the candidate State. That agreement shall be subject to ratification by each contracting State, in accordance with its respective constitutional requirements.

Article 58 SUSPENSION OF UNION MEMBERSHIP RIGHTS

1. On a reasoned proposal by one third of the Member States, by the European Parliament or by the Commission, the Council of Ministers, acting by a majority of four fifths of its members after obtaining the consent of the European Parliament, may adopt a European decision determining that there is a clear risk of a serious breach by a Member State of the values mentioned in Article 2. Before making such a determination, the Council of Ministers shall hear the Member State in question and, acting in accordance with the same procedure, may address recommendations to that State.

The Council of Ministers shall regularly verify that the grounds on which such a determination was made continue to apply.

2. The European Council, acting by unanimity on a proposal by one third of the Member States or by the Commission and after obtaining the consent of the European Parliament, may adopt a European decision determining the existence of a serious and persistent breach by a Member State of the values mentioned in Article 2, after inviting the Member State in question to submit its observations.

3.   Where a determination under paragraph 2 has been made, the Council of Ministers, acting by a qualified majority, may adopt a European decision suspending certain of the rights deriving from the application of the Constitution to the Member State in question, including the voting rights of that Member State in the Council of Ministers. In so doing, the Council of Ministers shall take into account the possible consequences of such a suspension on the rights and obligations of natural and legal persons.

That Member State shall in any case continue to be bound by its obligations under the Constitution.

4.   The Council of Ministers, acting by a qualified majority, may subsequently adopt a European decision varying or revoking measures taken under paragraph 3 in response to changes in the situation which led to their being imposed.

5.   For the purposes of this Article, the Council of Ministers shall act without taking into account the vote of the Member State in question. Abstentions by members present in person or represented shall not prevent the adoption of decisions referred to in paragraph 2.

This paragraph shall also apply in the event of voting rights being suspended pursuant to paragraph 3.

6.   For the purposes of paragraphs 1 and 2, the European Parliament shall act by a two-thirds majority of the votes cast, representing the majority of its Members.

Article 59   VOLUNTARY WITHDRAWAL FROM THE UNION

1.   Any Member State may decide to withdraw from the European Union in accordance with its own constitutional requirements.

2.   A Member State which decides to withdraw shall notify the European Council of its intention; the European Council shall examine that notification. In the light of the guidelines provided by the European Council, the Union shall negotiate and conclude an agreement with that State, setting out the arrangements for its withdrawal, taking account of the framework for its future relationship with the Union. That agreement shall be concluded on behalf of the Union by the Council of Ministers, acting by a qualified majority, after obtaining the consent of the European Parliament.

The representative of the withdrawing Member State shall not participate in Council of Ministers or European Council discussions or decisions concerning it.

3.   The Constitution shall cease to apply to the State in question from the date of entry into force of the withdrawal agreement or, failing that, two years after the notification referred to in paragraph 2, unless the European Council, in agreement with the Member State concerned, decides to extend this period.

4.   If a State which has withdrawn from the Union asks to re-join, its request shall be subject to the procedure referred to in Article 57.

PART II

THE CHARTER OF FUNDAMENTAL RIGHTS OF THE UNION

PREAMBLE

The peoples of Europe, in creating an ever closer union among them, are resolved to share a peaceful future based on common values.

Conscious of its spiritual and moral heritage, the Union is founded on the indivisible, universal values of human dignity, freedom, equality and solidarity; it is based on the principles of democracy and the rule of law. It places the individual at the heart of its activities, by establishing the citizenship of the Union and by creating an area of freedom, security and justice. The Union contributes to the preservation and to the development of these common values while respecting the diversity of the cultures and traditions of the peoples of Europe as well as the national identities of the Member States and the organisation of their public authorities at national, regional and local levels; it seeks to promote balanced and sustainable development and ensures free movement of persons, goods, services and capital, and the freedom of establishment.

To this end, it is necessary to strengthen the protection of fundamental rights in the light of changes in society, social progress and scientific and technological developments by making those rights more visible in a Charter.

This Charter reaffirms, with due regard for the powers and tasks of the Union and the principle of subsidiarity, the rights as they result, in particular, from the constitutional traditions and international obligations common to the Member States, the European Convention for the Protection of Human Rights and Fundamental Freedoms, the Social Charters adopted by the Union and by the Council of Europe and the case law of the Court of Justice of the European Union and of the European Court of Human Rights. In this context the Charter will be interpreted by the courts of the Union and the Member States with due regard to the explanations prepared at the instigation of the Praesidium of the Convention which drafted the Charter.

Enjoyment of these rights entails responsibilities and duties with regard to other persons, to the human community and to future generations.

The Union therefore recognises the rights, freedoms and principles set out hereafter.

Title I	# DIGNITY

Article II-1   ## HUMAN DIGNITY

Human dignity is inviolable. It must be respected and protected.

Article II-2   ## RIGHT TO LIFE

1.   Everyone has the right to life.

2.   No one shall be condemned to the death penalty, or executed.

Article II-3   ## RIGHT TO THE INTEGRITY OF THE PERSON

1.   Everyone has the right to respect for his or her physical and mental integrity.

2.   In the fields of medicine and biology, the following must be respected in particular:

(a) the free and informed consent of the person concerned, according to the procedures laid down by law,
(b) the prohibition of eugenic practices, in particular those aiming at the selection of persons,
(c) the prohibition on making the human body and its parts as such a source of financial gain,
(d) the prohibition of the reproductive cloning of human beings.

Article II-4   ## PROHIBITION OF TORTURE AND INHUMAN OR DEGRADING TREATMENT OR PUNISHMENT

No one shall be subjected to torture or to inhuman or degrading treatment or punishment.

Article II-5   PROHIBITION OF SLAVERY AND FORCED LABOUR

1.   No one shall be held in slavery or servitude.

2.   No one shall be required to perform forced or compulsory labour.

3.   Trafficking in human beings is prohibited.

Title II   FREEDOMS

Title II

Article II-6   RIGHT TO LIBERTY AND SECURITY

Everyone has the right to liberty and security of person.

Article II-7   RESPECT FOR PRIVATE AND FAMILY LIFE

Everyone has the right to respect for his or her private and family life, home and communications.

Article II-8   PROTECTION OF PERSONAL DATA

1.   Everyone has the right to the protection of personal data concerning him or her.

2.   Such data must be processed fairly for specified purposes and on the basis of the consent of the person concerned or some other legitimate basis laid down by law. Everyone has the right of access to data which has been collected concerning him or her, and the right to have it rectified.

3.   Compliance with these rules shall be subject to control by an independent authority.

Article II-9   RIGHT TO MARRY AND RIGHT TO FOUND A FAMILY

The right to marry and the right to found a family shall be guaranteed in accordance with the national laws governing the exercise of these rights.

Article II-10   FREEDOM OF THOUGHT, CONSCIENCE AND RELIGION

1.   Everyone has the right to freedom of thought, conscience and religion. This right includes freedom to change religion or belief and freedom, either alone or in

community with others and in public or in private, to manifest religion or belief, in worship, teaching, practice and observance.

2.   The right to conscientious objection is recognised, in accordance with the national laws governing the exercise of this right.

Article II-11   FREEDOM OF EXPRESSION AND INFORMATION

1.   Everyone has the right to freedom of expression. This right shall include freedom to hold opinions and to receive and impart information and ideas without interference by public authority and regardless of frontiers.

2.   The freedom and pluralism of the media shall be respected.

Article II-12   FREEDOM OF ASSEMBLY AND OF ASSOCIATION

1.   Everyone has the right to freedom of peaceful assembly and to freedom of association at all levels, in particular in political, trade union and civic matters, which implies the right of everyone to form and to join trade unions for the protection of his or her interests.

2.   Political parties at Union level contribute to expressing the political will of the citizens of the Union.

Article II-13   FREEDOM OF THE ARTS AND SCIENCES

The arts and scientific research shall be free of constraint. Academic freedom shall be respected.

Article II-14   RIGHT TO EDUCATION

1.   Everyone has the right to education and to have access to vocational and continuing training.

2.   This right includes the possibility to receive free compulsory education.

3.   The freedom to found educational establishments with due respect for democratic principles and the right of parents to ensure the education and teaching of their children in conformity with their religious, philosophical and pedagogical convictions shall be respected, in accordance with the national laws governing the exercise of such freedom and right.

Article II-15   FREEDOM TO CHOOSE AN OCCUPATION AND RIGHT TO ENGAGE IN WORK

1.   Everyone has the right to engage in work and to pursue a freely chosen or accepted occupation.

2.   Every citizen of the Union has the freedom to seek employment, to work, to exercise the right of establishment and to provide services in any Member State.

3.   Nationals of third countries who are authorised to work in the territories of the Member States are entitled to working conditions equivalent to those of citizens of the Union.

Article II-16   FREEDOM TO CONDUCT A BUSINESS

The freedom to conduct a business in accordance with Union law and national laws and practices is recognised.

Article II-17   RIGHT TO PROPERTY

1.   Everyone has the right to own, use, dispose of and bequeath his or her lawfully acquired possessions. No one may be deprived of his or her possessions, except in the public interest and in the cases and under the conditions provided for by law, subject to fair compensation being paid in good time for their loss. The use of property may be regulated by law insofar as is necessary for the general interest.

2.   Intellectual property shall be protected.

Article II-18   RIGHT TO ASYLUM

The right to asylum shall be guaranteed with due respect for the rules of the Geneva Convention of 28 July 1951 and the Protocol of 31 January 1967 relating to the status of refugees and in accordance with the Constitution.

Article II-19   PROTECTION IN THE EVENT OF REMOVAL, EXPULSION OR EXTRADITION

1.   Collective expulsions are prohibited.

2.   No one may be removed, expelled or extradited to a State where there is a serious risk that he or she would be subjected to the death penalty, torture or other inhuman or degrading treatment or punishment.

Title III   EQUALITY

Article II-20   EQUALITY BEFORE THE LAW

Everyone is equal before the law.

Article II-21   NON-DISCRIMINATION

1.   Any discrimination based on any ground such as sex, race, colour, ethnic or social origin, genetic features, language, religion or belief, political or any other opinion, membership of a national minority, property, birth, disability, age or sexual orientation shall be prohibited.

2.   Within the scope of application of the Constitution and without prejudice to any of its specific provisions, any discrimination on grounds of nationality shall be prohibited.

Article II-22   CULTURAL, RELIGIOUS AND LINGUISTIC DIVERSITY

The Union shall respect cultural, religious and linguistic diversity.

Article II-23   EQUALITY BETWEEN MEN AND WOMEN

Equality between men and women must be ensured in all areas, including employment, work and pay.

The principle of equality shall not prevent the maintenance or adoption of measures providing for specific advantages in favour of the under-represented sex.

Article II-24   THE RIGHTS OF THE CHILD

1.   Children shall have the right to such protection and care as is necessary for their well-being. They may express their views freely. Such views shall be taken into consideration on matters which concern them in accordance with their age and maturity.

2.   In all actions relating to children, whether taken by public authorities or private Institutions, the child's best interests must be a primary consideration.

3.   Every child shall have the right to maintain on a regular basis a personal relationship and direct contact with both his or her parents, unless that is contrary to his or her interests.

Article II-25   THE RIGHTS OF THE ELDERLY

The Union recognises and respects the rights of the elderly to lead a life of dignity and independence and to participate in social and cultural life.

Article II-26   INTEGRATION OF PERSONS WITH DISABILITIES

The Union recognises and respects the right of persons with disabilities to benefit from measures designed to ensure their independence, social and occupational integration and participation in the life of the community.

Title IV — SOLIDARITY

Article II-27 WORKERS' RIGHT TO INFORMATION AND CONSULTATION WITHIN THE UNDERTAKING

Workers or their representatives must, at the appropriate levels, be guaranteed information and consultation in good time in the cases and under the conditions provided for by Union law and national laws and practices.

Article II-28 RIGHT OF COLLECTIVE BARGAINING AND ACTION

Workers and employers, or their respective organisations, have, in accordance with Union law and national laws and practices, the right to negotiate and conclude collective agreements at the appropriate levels and, in cases of conflicts of interest, to take collective action to defend their interests, including strike action.

Article II-29 RIGHT OF ACCESS TO PLACEMENT SERVICES

Everyone has the right of access to a free placement service.

Article II-30 PROTECTION IN THE EVENT OF UNJUSTIFIED DISMISSAL

Every worker has the right to protection against unjustified dismissal, in accordance with Union law and national laws and practices.

Article II-31 FAIR AND JUST WORKING CONDITIONS

1. Every worker has the right to working conditions which respect his or her health, safety and dignity.

2. Every worker has the right to limitation of maximum working hours, to daily and weekly rest periods and to an annual period of paid leave.

Article II-32 PROHIBITION OF CHILD LABOUR AND PROTECTION OF YOUNG PEOPLE AT WORK

The employment of children is prohibited. The minimum age of admission to employment may not be lower than the minimum school-leaving age, without prejudice to such rules as may be more favourable to young people and except for limited derogations.

Young people admitted to work must have working conditions appropriate to their age and be protected against economic exploitation and any work likely to harm their safety, health or physical, mental, moral or social development or to interfere with their education.

Article II-33 FAMILY AND PROFESSIONAL LIFE

1.	The family shall enjoy legal, economic and social protection.

2.	To reconcile family and professional life, everyone shall have the right to protection from dismissal for a reason connected with maternity and the right to paid maternity leave and to parental leave following the birth or adoption of a child.

Article II-34 SOCIAL SECURITY AND SOCIAL ASSISTANCE

1.	The Union recognises and respects the entitlement to social security benefits and social services providing protection in cases such as maternity, illness, industrial accidents, dependency or old age, and in the case of loss of employment, in accordance with the rules laid down by Union law and national laws and practices.

2.	Everyone residing and moving legally within the European Union is entitled to social security benefits and social advantages in accordance with Union law and national laws and practices.

3.	In order to combat social exclusion and poverty, the Union recognises and respects the right to social and housing assistance so as to ensure a decent existence for all those who lack sufficient resources, in accordance with the rules laid down by Union law and national laws and practices.

Article II-35   HEALTH CARE

Everyone has the right of access to preventive health care and the right to benefit from medical treatment under the conditions established by national laws and practices. A high level of human health protection shall be ensured in the definition and implementation of all Union policies and activities.

Article II-36   ACCESS TO SERVICES OF GENERAL ECONOMIC INTEREST

The Union recognises and respects access to services of general economic interest as provided for in national laws and practices, in accordance with the Constitution, in order to promote the social and territorial cohesion of the Union.

Article II-37   ENVIRONMENTAL PROTECTION

A high level of environmental protection and the improvement of the quality of the environment must be integrated into the policies of the Union and ensured in accordance with the principle of sustainable development.

Article II-38   CONSUMER PROTECTION

Union policies shall ensure a high level of consumer protection.

CITIZENS' RIGHTS

Article II-39 **RIGHT TO VOTE AND TO STAND AS A CANDIDATE AT ELECTIONS TO THE EUROPEAN PARLIAMENT**

1.	Every citizen of the Union has the right to vote and to stand as a candidate at elections to the European Parliament in the Member State in which he or she resides, under the same conditions as nationals of that State.

2.	Members of the European Parliament shall be elected by direct universal suffrage in a free and secret ballot.

Article II-40 **RIGHT TO VOTE AND TO STAND AS A CANDIDATE AT MUNICIPAL ELECTIONS**

Every citizen of the Union has the right to vote and to stand as a candidate at municipal elections in the Member State in which he or she resides under the same conditions as nationals of that State.

Article II-41 **RIGHT TO GOOD ADMINISTRATION**

1.	Every person has the right to have his or her affairs handled impartially, fairly and within a reasonable time by the Institutions, bodies and agencies of the Union.

2.	This right includes:

(a) the right of every person to be heard, before any individual measure which would affect him or her adversely is taken;
(b) the right of every person to have access to his or her file, while respecting the legitimate interests of confidentiality and of professional and business secrecy;
(c) the obligation of the administration to give reasons for its decisions.

3.　　　　Every person has the right to have the Union make good any damage caused by its Institutions or by its servants in the performance of their duties, in accordance with the general principles common to the laws of the Member States.

4.　　　　Every person may write to the Institutions of the Union in one of the languages of the Constitution and must have an answer in the same language.

Article II-42　RIGHT OF ACCESS TO DOCUMENTS

Any citizen of the Union, and any natural or legal person residing or having its registered office in a Member State, has a right of access to documents of the Institutions, bodies and agencies of the Union, in whatever form they are produced.

Article II-43　EUROPEAN OMBUDSMAN

Any citizen of the Union and any natural or legal person residing or having its registered office in a Member State has the right to refer to the European Ombudsman cases of maladministration in the activities of the Institutions, bodies or agencies of the Union, with the exception of the European Court of Justice and the High Court acting in their judicial role.

Article II-44　RIGHT TO PETITION

Any citizen of the Union and any natural or legal person residing or having its registered office in a Member State has the right to petition the European Parliament.

Article II-45　FREEDOM OF MOVEMENT AND OF RESIDENCE

1.　　　　Every citizen of the Union has the right to move and reside freely within the territory of the Member States.

2.　　　　Freedom of movement and residence may be granted, in accordance with the Constitution, to nationals of third countries legally resident in the territory of a Member State.

Article II-46 DIPLOMATIC AND CONSULAR PROTECTION

Every citizen of the Union shall, in the territory of a third country in which the Member State of which he or she is a national is not represented, be entitled to protection by the diplomatic or consular authorities of any Member State, on the same conditions as the nationals of that Member State.

Article II-47 RIGHT TO AN EFFECTIVE REMEDY AND TO A FAIR TRIAL

Everyone whose rights and freedoms guaranteed by the law of the Union are violated has the right to an effective remedy before a tribunal in compliance with the conditions laid down in this Article.

Everyone is entitled to a fair and public hearing within a reasonable time by an independent and impartial tribunal previously established by law. Everyone shall have the possibility of being advised, defended and represented.

Legal aid shall be made available to those who lack sufficient resources insofar as such aid is necessary to ensure effective access to justice.

Article II-48 PRESUMPTION OF INNOCENCE AND RIGHT OF DEFENCE

1.   Everyone who has been charged shall be presumed innocent until proved guilty according to law.

2.   Respect for the rights of the defence of anyone who has been charged shall be guaranteed.

Article II-49 PRINCIPLES OF LEGALITY AND PROPORTIONALITY OF CRIMINAL OFFENCES AND PENALTIES

1.   No one shall be held guilty of any criminal offence on account of any act or omission which did not constitute a criminal offence under national law or international law at the time when it was committed. Nor shall a heavier penalty be imposed than that which was applicable at the time the criminal offence was committed. If, subsequent to the commission of a criminal offence, the law provides for a lighter penalty, that penalty shall be applicable.

2.   This Article shall not prejudice the trial and punishment of any person for any act or omission which, at the time when it was committed, was criminal according to the general principles recognised by the community of nations.

3.   The severity of penalties must not be disproportionate to the criminal offence.

Article II-50   RIGHT NOT TO BE TRIED OR PUNISHED TWICE IN
                CRIMINAL PROCEEDINGS FOR THE SAME CRIMINAL
                OFFENCE

No one shall be liable to be tried or punished again in criminal proceedings for an offence for which he or she has already been finally acquitted or convicted within the Union in accordance with the law.

GENERAL PROVISIONS GOVERNING THE INTERPRETATION AND APPLICATION OF THE CHARTER

Title VII

Article II-51   FIELD OF APPLICATION

1.   The provisions of this Charter are addressed to the Institutions, bodies and agencies of the Union with due regard for the principle of subsidiarity and to the Member States only when they are implementing Union law. They shall therefore respect the rights, observe the principles and promote the application thereof in accordance with their respective powers and respecting the limits of the powers of the Union as conferred on it in the other Parts of the Constitution.

2.   This Charter does not extend the field of application of Union law beyond the powers of the Union or establish any new power or task for the Union, or modify powers and tasks defined in the other Parts of the Constitution.

Article II-52   SCOPE AND INTERPRETATION
              OF RIGHTS AND PRINCIPLES

1.   Any limitation on the exercise of the rights and freedoms recognised by this Charter must be provided for by law and respect the essence of those rights and freedoms. Subject to the principle of proportionality, limitations may be made only if they are necessary and genuinely meet objectives of general interest recognised by the Union or the need to protect the rights and freedoms of others.

2.   Rights recognised by this Charter for which provision is made in other Parts of the Constitution shall be exercised under the conditions and within the limits defined by these relevant Parts.

3.   Insofar as this Charter contains rights which correspond to rights guaranteed by the Convention for the Protection of Human Rights and Fundamental Freedoms, the meaning and scope of those rights shall be the same as those laid down by the said Convention. This provision shall not prevent Union law providing more extensive protection.

4.　　　　Insofar as this Charter recognises fundamental rights as they result from the constitutional traditions common to the Member States, those rights shall be interpreted in harmony with those traditions.

5.　　　　The provisions of this Charter which contain principles may be implemented by legislative and executive acts taken by Institutions and bodies of the Union, and by acts of Member States when they are implementing Union law, in the exercise of their respective powers. They shall be judicially cognisable only in the interpretation of such acts and in the ruling on their legality.

6.　　　　Full account shall be taken of national laws and practices as specified in this Charter.

Article II-53 LEVEL OF PROTECTION

Nothing in this Charter shall be interpreted as restricting or adversely affecting human rights and fundamental freedoms as recognised, in their respective fields of application, by Union law and international law and by international agreements to which the Union or all the Member States are party, including the European Convention for the Protection of Human Rights and Fundamental Freedoms, and by the Member States' constitutions.

Article II-54 PROHIBITION OF ABUSE OF RIGHTS

Nothing in this Charter shall be interpreted as implying any right to engage in any activity or to perform any act aimed at the destruction of any of the rights and freedoms recognised in this Charter or at their limitation to a greater extent than is provided for herein.

PART III

THE POLICIES
AND FUNCTIONING
OF THE UNION

CLAUSES OF GENERAL APPLICATION

Article III-1

The Union shall ensure consistency between the different policies and activities referred to in this Part, taking all of the Union's objectives into account and in accordance with the principle of conferring of powers.

Article III-2

In all the activities referred to in this Part, the Union shall aim to eliminate inequalities, and to promote equality, between men and women.

Article III-3

In defining and implementing the policies and activities referred to in this Part, the Union shall aim to combat discrimination based on sex, racial or ethnic origin, religion or belief, disability, age or sexual orientation.

Article III-4

Environmental protection requirements must be integrated into the definition and implementation of the Union policies and activities referred to in this Part, in particular with a view to promoting sustainable development.

Article III-5

Consumer protection requirements shall be taken into account in defining and implementing other Union policies and activities.

Article III-6

Without prejudice to Articles III-55, III-56 and III-136, and given the place occupied by services of general economic interest as services to which all in the Union attribute value as well as their role in promoting social and territorial cohesion, the Union and the Member States, each within their respective powers and within the scope of application of the Constitution, shall take care that such services operate on the basis of principles and conditions, in particular economic and financial, which enable them to fulfil their missions. European laws shall define these principles and conditions.

Title II NON-DISCRIMINATION AND CITIZENSHIP

Article III-7

European laws or framework laws may lay down rules to prohibit discrimination on grounds of nationality as referred to in Article I-4.

Article III-8

1.   Without prejudice to the other provisions of the Constitution and within the limits of the powers conferred by it upon the Union, a European law or framework law of the Council of Ministers may establish the measures needed to combat discrimination based on sex, racial or ethnic origin, religion or belief, disability, age or sexual orientation. The Council of Ministers shall act unanimously after obtaining the consent of the European Parliament.

2.   European laws or framework laws may establish basic principles for Union incentive measures and define such incentive measures, to support action taken by Member States, excluding any harmonisation of their laws and regulations.

Article III-9

1.   If action by the Union should prove necessary to facilitate the exercise of the right, referred to in Article I-8, of every Union citizen to move and reside freely and the Constitution has not provided the necessary powers, European laws or framework laws may establish measures for that purpose.

2.   For the same purpose and unless the Constitution has provided for powers of action in this area, measures concerning passports, identity cards, residence permits or any other such document and measures concerning social security or social protection may be laid down by a European law or framework law of the Council of Ministers. The Council of Ministers shall act unanimously after consulting the European Parliament.

Article III-10

A European law or framework law of the Council of Ministers shall determine the detailed arrangements for exercising the right, referred to in Article I-8, for every Union citizen to vote and to stand as a candidate in municipal elections and elections to the European Parliament in their Member State of residence without being a national of that State. The Council of Ministers shall act unanimously after consulting the European Parliament. These arrangements may provide for derogations where warranted by problems specific to a Member State.

The right to vote and to stand as a candidate in elections to the European Parliament shall be exercised without prejudice to Article III-232(2) and the measures adopted for its implementation.

Article III-11

Member States shall adopt the necessary provisions to secure diplomatic and consular protection of citizens of the Union in third countries, as referred to in Article I-8.

A European law of the Council of Ministers may establish the measures necessary to facilitate such protection. The Council of Ministers shall act after consulting the European Parliament.

Article III-12

The languages in which every citizen of the Union has the right to address the institutions or advisory bodies under Article I-8, and to have an answer, are those listed in Article IV-10. The institutions and advisory bodies referred to in this Article are those listed in Articles I-18(2), I-30 and I-31 and also the European Ombudsman.

Article III-13

The Commission shall report to the European Parliament, to the Council of Ministers and to the Economic and Social Committee every three years on the application of the provisions of Article I-8 and of this Title. This report shall take account of the development of the Union.

On this basis, and without prejudice to the other provisions of the Constitution, a European law or framework law of the Council of Ministers may add to the rights laid down in Article I-8. The Council of Ministers shall act unanimously after obtaining the consent of the European Parliament. The law or framework law concerned shall not enter into force until it is approved by the Member States in accordance with their respective constitutional requirements.

Article III-14

1.   The Union shall adopt measures with the aim of establishing the internal market, in accordance with this Article, Article III-15, Article III-26(1) and Articles III-29, III-39, III-62, III-65 and III-143 and without prejudice to the other provisions of the Constitution.

2.   The internal market shall comprise an area without internal frontiers in which the free movement of goods, persons, services and capital is ensured in accordance with the Constitution.

3.   The Council of Ministers, on a proposal from the Commission, shall adopt European regulations and decisions determining the guidelines and conditions necessary to ensure balanced progress in all the sectors concerned.

Article III-15

When drawing up its proposals with a view to achieving the objectives set out in Article III-14, the Commission shall take into account the extent of the effort that certain economies showing differences in development will have to sustain for the establishment of the internal market and it may propose appropriate measures.

If these measures take the form of derogations, they must be of a temporary nature and must cause the least possible disturbance to the functioning of the internal market.

Article III-16

Member States shall consult each other with a view to taking together the steps needed to prevent the functioning of the internal market being affected by steps which a Member State may be called upon to take in the event of serious internal disturbances affecting the maintenance of law and order, in the event of war, serious international tension constituting a threat of war, or in order to carry out obligations it has accepted for the purpose of maintaining peace and international security.

Article III-17

If steps taken in the circumstances referred to in Articles III-6 and III-34 have the effect of distorting the conditions of competition in the internal market, the Commission shall, together with the State concerned, examine how these steps can be adjusted to the rules laid down in the Constitution.

By way of derogation from the procedure laid down in Articles III-265 and III-266, the Commission or any Member State may bring the matter directly before the Court of Justice if it considers that another Member State is making improper use of the powers provided for in Articles III-6 and III-34. The Court of Justice shall give its ruling in camera.

Section 2   FREE MOVEMENT OF PERSONS AND SERVICES

Subsection 1   WORKERS

Article III-18

1.   Workers shall have the right to move freely within the Union.

2.   Any discrimination based on nationality between workers of the Member States as regards employment, remuneration and other conditions of work and employment shall be prohibited.

3.   Workers shall have the right, subject to limitations justified on grounds of public policy, public security or public health:

(a) to accept offers of employment actually made;
(b) to move freely within the territory of Member States for this purpose;
(c) to stay in a Member State for the purpose of employment in accordance with the provisions governing the employment of nationals of that State laid down by law, regulation or administrative action;
(d) to remain in the territory of a Member State after having been employed in that State, subject to conditions which shall be embodied in European regulations adopted by the Commission.

4.   This Article shall not apply to employment in the public service.

Article III-19

European laws or framework laws shall establish the measures needed to bring about freedom of movement for workers, as defined in Article III-18. They shall be adopted after consultation of the Economic and Social Committee.

Such European laws or framework laws shall aim, in particular, to:

(a) ensure close cooperation between national employment services;
(b) abolish those administrative procedures and practices and those qualifying periods in respect of eligibility for available employment, whether resulting from national legislation or from agreements previously concluded between Member States, the maintenance of which would form an obstacle to liberalisation of the movement of workers;
(c) abolish all such qualifying periods and other restrictions provided for either under national legislation or under agreements previously concluded between Member States as impose on workers of other Member States conditions regarding the free choice of employment other than those imposed on workers of the State concerned;
(d) set up appropriate machinery to bring offers of employment into touch with applications for employment and to facilitate the achievement of a balance between supply and demand in the employment market in such a way as to avoid serious threats to the standard of living and level of employment in the various regions and industries.

Article III-20

Member States shall, within the framework of a joint programme, encourage the exchange of young workers.

Article III-21

In the field of social security, European laws or framework laws shall establish such measures as are necessary to bring about freedom of movement for workers by introducing a system to secure for employed and self-employed migrant workers and their dependants:

(a) aggregation, for the purpose of acquiring and retaining the right to benefit and of calculating the amount of benefit, of all periods taken into account under the laws of the several countries;

(b) payment of benefits to persons resident in the territories of Member States.

Subsection 2 FREEDOM OF ESTABLISHMENT

Article III-22

Within the framework of this Subsection, restrictions on the freedom of establishment of nationals of a Member State in the territory of another Member State shall be prohibited. Such prohibition shall also apply to restrictions on the setting-up of agencies, branches or subsidiaries by nationals of any Member State established in the territory of any Member State.

Nationals of a Member State shall have the right, in the territory of another Member State, to take up and pursue activities as self-employed persons and to set up and manage undertakings, in particular companies or firms within the meaning of the second paragraph of Article III-27, under the conditions laid down for its own nationals by the law of the Member State where such establishment is effected, subject to the provisions of the Section relating to capital.

1.   European framework laws shall establish measures in order to attain freedom of establishment as regards a particular activity. They shall be adopted after consultation of the Economic and Social Committee.

2.   The European Parliament, the Council of Ministers and the Commission
shall carry out the duties devolving upon them under paragraph 1, in particular:

    (a) by according, as a general rule, priority treatment to activities where
        freedom of establishment makes a particularly valuable contribution to
        the development of production and trade;

    (b) by ensuring close cooperation between the competent authorities in the
        Member States in order to ascertain the particular situation within the
        Union of the various activities concerned;

    (c) by abolishing those administrative procedures and practices, whether
        resulting from national legislation or from agreements previously con-
        cluded between Member States, the maintenance of which would form
        an obstacle to freedom of establishment;

    (d) by ensuring that workers from one Member State employed in the ter-
        ritory of another Member State may remain in that territory for the pur-
        pose of taking up activities therein as self-employed persons, where they
        satisfy the conditions which they would be required to satisfy if they were
        entering that State at the time when they intended to take up such acti-
        vities;

    (e) by enabling a national of one Member State to acquire and use land and
        buildings situated in the territory of another Member State, insofar as
        this does not conflict with the principles laid down in Article III-123(2);

    (f) by effecting the progressive abolition of restrictions on freedom of estab-
        lishment in every branch of activity under consideration, both as regards
        the conditions for setting up agencies, branches or subsidiaries in the ter-
        ritory of a Member State and as regards the conditions governing the
        entry of personnel belonging to the main establishment into managerial
        or supervisory posts in such agencies, branches or subsidiaries;

    (g) by coordinating to the necessary extent the safeguards which, for the
        protection of the interests of members and others, are required by
        Member States of companies or firms within the meaning of the second
        paragraph of Article III-27 with a view to making such safeguards equiv-
        alent throughout the Union;

(h) by satisfying themselves that the conditions of establishment are not distorted by aids granted by Member States.

Article III-24

This Subsection shall not apply, so far as any given Member State is concerned, to activities which in that State are connected, even occasionally, with the exercise of official authority.

European laws or framework laws may exempt certain activities from application of this Subsection.

Article III-25

1.   This Subsection and measures adopted in pursuance thereof shall not prejudice the applicability of provisions laid down by law, regulation or administrative action in Member States providing for special treatment for foreign nationals on grounds of public policy, public security or public health.

2.   European framework laws shall coordinate the national provisions referred to in paragraph 1.

Article III-26

1.   European framework laws shall make it easier for persons to take up and pursue activities as self-employed persons. They shall cover:

(a) the mutual recognition of diplomas, certificates and other evidence of formal qualifications;
(b) the coordination of the provisions laid down by law, regulation or administrative action in Member States concerning the taking-up and pursuit of activities as self-employed persons.

2.   In the case of the medical and allied and pharmaceutical professions, the progressive abolition of restrictions shall be dependent upon coordination of the conditions for their exercise in the various Member States.

Article III-27

Companies or firms formed in accordance with the law of a Member State and having their registered office, central administration or principal place of business within the Union shall, for the purposes of this Subsection, be treated in the same way as natural persons who are nationals of Member States.

"Companies or firms" means companies or firms constituted under civil or commercial law, including cooperative societies, and other legal persons governed by public or private law, save for those which are non-profit-making.

Article III-28

Member States shall accord nationals of the other Member States the same treatment as their own nationals as regards participation in the capital of companies or firms within the meaning of Article III-27, without prejudice to the application of the other provisions of the Constitution.

Subsection 3   FREEDOM TO PROVIDE SERVICES

Article III-29

Within the framework of this Subsection, restrictions on freedom to provide services within the Union shall be prohibited in respect of nationals of Member States who are established in a Member State other than that of the person for whom the services are intended.

European laws or framework laws may extend this Subsection to nationals of a third country who provide services and who are established within the Union.

Article III-30

Services shall be considered to be "services" within the meaning of the Constitution where they are normally provided for remuneration, insofar as they are not governed by the provisions relating to freedom of movement for goods, capital and persons.

"Services" shall in particular include:

> (a) activities of an industrial character;
> (b) activities of a commercial character;
> (c) activities of craftsmen;
> (d) activities of the professions.

Without prejudice to the Subsection relating to the right of establishment, the person providing a service may, in order to do so, temporarily pursue his or her activity in the Member State where the service is provided, under the same conditions as are imposed by that State on its own nationals.

Article III-31

1.   Freedom to provide services in the field of transport shall be governed by the Section relating to transport.

2.   The liberalisation of banking and insurance services connected with movements of capital shall be effected in step with the liberalisation of movement of capital.

Article III-32

1.   A European framework law shall establish the measures in order to achieve the liberalisation of a specific service. It shall be adopted after consultation of the Economic and Social Committee.

2.   As regards the European framework law referred to in paragraph 1, priority shall as a general rule be given to those services which directly affect production costs or the liberalisation of which helps to promote trade in goods.

Article III-33

The Member States declare their readiness to undertake the liberalisation of services beyond the extent required by the European framework law adopted pursuant to Article III-32(1), if their general economic situation and the situation of the economic sector concerned so permit.

To this end, the Commission shall make recommendations to the Member States concerned.

Article III-34

As long as restrictions on freedom to provide services have not been abolished, each Member State shall apply such restrictions without distinction on grounds of nationality or of residence to all persons providing services within the meaning of the first paragraph of Article III-29.

Article III-35

Articles III-24 to III-27 shall apply to the matters covered by this Subsection.

Section 3 FREE MOVEMENT OF GOODS

Subsection 1 CUSTOMS UNION

Article III-36

1.	The Union shall comprise a customs union which shall cover all trade in goods and which shall involve the prohibition between Member States of customs duties on imports and exports and of all charges having equivalent effect, and the adoption of a common customs tariff in their relations with third countries.

2.	Article III-38 and Subsection 3 of this Section shall apply to products originating in Member States and to products coming from third countries which are in free circulation in Member States.

Article III-37

Products coming from a third country shall be considered to be in free circulation in a Member State if the import formalities have been complied with and any customs duties or charges having equivalent effect which are payable have been levied in that Member State, and if they have not benefited from a total or partial drawback of such duties or charges.

Article III-38

Customs duties on imports and exports and charges having equivalent effect shall be prohibited between Member States. This prohibition shall also apply to customs duties of a fiscal nature.

Article III-39

The Council of Ministers, on a proposal from the Commission, shall adopt the European regulations and decisions fixing Common Customs Tariff duties.

Article III-40

In carrying out the tasks entrusted to it under this Subsection the Commission shall be guided by:

(a) the need to promote trade between Member States and third countries;
(b) developments in conditions of competition within the Union insofar as they lead to an improvement in the competitive capacity of undertakings;
(c) the requirements of the Union as regards the supply of raw materials and semi-finished goods; in this connection the Commission shall take care to avoid distorting conditions of competition between Member States in respect of finished goods;
(d) the need to avoid serious disturbances in the economies of Member States and to ensure rational development of production and an expansion of consumption within the Union.

CUSTOMS COOPERATION

Article III-41

Within the scope of application of the Constitution, European laws or framework laws shall establish measures in order to strengthen customs cooperation between Member States and between the latter and the Commission.

Subsection 3 PROHIBITION OF QUANTITATIVE RESTRICTIONS

Article III-42

Quantitative restrictions on imports and exports and all measures having equivalent effect shall be prohibited between Member States.

Article III-43

Article III-42 shall not preclude prohibitions or restrictions on imports, exports or goods in transit justified on grounds of public morality, public policy or public security; the protection of health and life of humans, animals or plants; the protection of national treasures possessing artistic, historic or archaeological value; or the protection of industrial and commercial property. Such prohibitions or restrictions shall not, however, constitute a means of arbitrary discrimination or a disguised restriction on trade between Member States.

Article III-44

1.   Member States shall adjust any State monopolies of a commercial character so as to ensure that no discrimination regarding the conditions under which goods are procured and marketed exists between nationals of Member States.

This Article shall apply to any body through which a Member State, in law or in fact, either directly or indirectly supervises, determines or appreciably influences imports or exports between Member States. It shall likewise apply to monopolies delegated by the State to others.

2. Member States shall refrain from any new step which is contrary to the principles laid down in paragraph 1 or which restricts the scope of the Articles dealing with the prohibition of customs duties and quantitative restrictions between Member States.

3. If a State monopoly of a commercial character has rules which are designed to make it easier to dispose of agricultural products or obtain for them the best return, steps should be taken in applying this Article to ensure equivalent safeguards for the employment and standard of living of the producers concerned.

Section 4 CAPITAL AND PAYMENTS

Article III-45

Within the framework of this Section, restrictions both on the movement of capital and on payments between Member States and between Member States and third countries shall be prohibited.

Article III-46

1. Article III-45 shall be without prejudice to the application to third countries of any restrictions which existed on 31 December 1993 under national or Union law adopted in respect of the movement of capital to or from third countries involving direct investment – including in real estate –, establishment, the provision of financial services or the admission of securities to capital markets.

2. European laws or framework laws shall enact measures on the movement of capital to or from third countries involving direct investment – including investment in real estate –, establishment, the provision of financial services or the admission of securities to capital markets.

The European Parliament and the Council of Ministers shall endeavour to achieve the objective of free movement of capital between Member States and third countries to the greatest extent possible and without prejudice to other provisions of the Constitution.

3.   Notwithstanding paragraph 2, only a European law or framework law of the Council of Ministers may enact measures which constitute a step back in Union law as regards the liberalisation of the movement of capital to or from third countries. The Council of Ministers shall act unanimously after consulting the European Parliament.

Article III-47

1.   Article III-45 shall be without prejudice to the right of Member States:

    (a) to apply the relevant provisions of their tax law which distinguish between taxpayers who are not in the same situation with regard to their place of residence or with regard to the place where their capital is invested;

    (b) to take all requisite steps to prevent infringements of national provisions laid down by law or regulation, in particular in the field of taxation and the prudential supervision of financial institutions, or to lay down procedures for the declaration of capital movements for purposes of administrative or statistical information, or to take steps which are justified on grounds of public policy or public security.

2.   This Section shall be without prejudice to the applicability of restrictions on the right of establishment which are compatible with the Constitution.

3.   The steps and procedures referred to in paragraphs 1 and 2 shall not constitute a means of arbitrary discrimination or a disguised restriction on the free movement of capital and payments as defined in Article III-45.

Article III-48

Where, in exceptional circumstances, movements of capital to or from third countries cause, or threaten to cause, serious difficulties for the operation of economic and monetary union, the Council of Ministers, on a proposal from the Commission, may adopt

European regulations or decisions introducing safeguard measures with regard to third countries for a period not exceeding six months if such measures are strictly necessary. It shall act after consulting the European Central Bank.

Article III-49

Where necessary to achieve the objectives set out in Article III-158, in particular as regards prevention of and fight against organised crime, terrorism and trafficking in human beings, European laws may define a framework for measures with regard to capital movements and payments, such as the freezing of funds, financial assets or economic gains belonging to, or owned or held by, natural or legal persons, groups or non-state entities.

The Council of Ministers, on a proposal from the Commission, shall adopt European regulations or European decisions in order to implement the laws referred to in the first paragraph.

Section 5 RULES ON COMPETITION

Subsection 1 RULES APPLYING TO UNDERTAKINGS

Article III-50

1. The following shall be prohibited as incompatible with the internal market: all agreements between undertakings, decisions by associations of undertakings and concerted practices which may affect trade between Member States and which have as their object or effect the prevention, restriction or distortion of competition within the internal market, and in particular those which:

(a) directly or indirectly fix purchase or selling prices or any other trading conditions;
(b) limit or control production, markets, technical development, or investment;
(c) share markets or sources of supply;

(d) apply dissimilar conditions to equivalent transactions with other trading parties, thereby placing them at a competitive disadvantage;

(e) make the conclusion of contracts subject to acceptance by the other parties of supplementary obligations which, by their nature or according to commercial usage, have no connection with the subject of such contracts.

2.   Any agreements or decisions prohibited pursuant to this Article shall be automatically void.

3.   Paragraph 1 may, however, be declared inapplicable in the case of:

   – any agreement or category of agreements between undertakings;
   – any decision or category of decisions by associations of undertakings;
   – any concerted practice or category of concerted practices,

which contributes to improving the production or distribution of goods or to promoting technical or economic progress, while allowing consumers a fair share of the resulting benefit, and which does not:

(a) impose on the undertakings concerned restrictions which are not indispensable to the attainment of these objectives;

(b) afford such undertakings the possibility of eliminating competition in respect of a substantial part of the products in question.

Article III-51

Any abuse by one or more undertakings of a dominant position within the internal market or in a substantial part of it shall be prohibited as incompatible with the internal market insofar as it may affect trade between Member States.

Such abuse may, in particular, consist in:

(a) directly or indirectly imposing unfair purchase or selling prices or other unfair trading conditions;

(b) limiting production, markets or technical development to the prejudice of consumers;

(c) applying dissimilar conditions to equivalent transactions with other trading parties, thereby placing them at a competitive disadvantage;

(d) making the conclusion of contracts subject to acceptance by the other parties of supplementary obligations which, by their nature or according to commercial usage, have no connection with the subject of such contracts.

Article III-52

1.   The Council of Ministers, on a proposal from the Commission, shall adopt the European regulations to give effect to the principles set out in Articles III-50 and III-51. It shall act after consulting the European Parliament.

2.   The European regulations referred to in paragraph 1 shall be designed in particular:

(a) to ensure compliance with the prohibitions laid down in Article III-50(1) and in Article III-51 by making provision for fines and periodic penalty payments;

(b) to lay down detailed rules for the application of Article III-50(3), taking into account the need to ensure effective supervision on the one hand, and to simplify administration to the greatest possible extent on the other;

(c) to define, if need be, in the various branches of the economy, the scope of the provisions of Articles III-50 and III-51;

(d) to define the respective functions of the Commission and of the Court of Justice in applying the provisions laid down in this paragraph;

(e) to determine the relationship between national laws and this Section or the European regulations adopted pursuant to this Article.

Article III-53

Until the entry into force of the European regulations adopted pursuant to Article III-52, the authorities in Member States shall rule on the admissibility of agreements, decisions and concerted practices and on abuse of a dominant position in the internal market in accordance with their internal law and Article III-50, in particular paragraph 3, and Article III-51.

Article III-54

1.   Without prejudice to Article III-53, the Commission shall ensure the application of the principles laid down in Articles III-50 and III-51. On application by a Member State or on its own initiative, and in cooperation with the competent authorities in the Member States, which shall give it their assistance, the Commission shall investigate cases of suspected infringement of these principles. If it finds that there has been an infringement, it shall propose appropriate measures to bring it to an end.

2.   If the infringement is not brought to an end, the Commission shall adopt a reasoned European decision recording the infringement of the principles. The Commission may publish its decision and authorise Member States to take the steps, the conditions and details of which it shall determine, needed to remedy the situation.

3.   The Commission may adopt European regulations relating to the categories of agreement in respect of which the Council of Ministers has acted pursuant to Article III-52(2)(b).

Article III-55

1.   In the case of public undertakings and undertakings to which Member States grant special or exclusive rights, Member States shall neither enact nor maintain in force any provision contrary to the provisions of the Constitution, in particular Article I-4(2) and Articles III-55 to III-58.

2.   Undertakings entrusted with the operation of services of general economic interest or having the character of a revenue-producing monopoly shall be subject to the provisions of the Constitution, in particular to the rules on competition, insofar as the application of such rules does not obstruct the performance, in law or in fact, of the particular tasks assigned to them. The development of trade must not be affected to such an extent as would be contrary to the Union's interests.

3.   The Commission shall ensure the application of this Article and shall, where necessary, adopt appropriate European regulations or decisions.

Article III-56

1.   Save as otherwise provided in the Constitution, any aid granted by a Member State or through State resources in any form whatsoever which distorts or threatens to distort competition by favouring certain undertakings or the production of certain goods shall, insofar as it affects trade between Member States, be incompatible with the internal market.

2.   The following shall be compatible with the internal market:

(a) aid having a social character, granted to individual consumers, provided that such aid is granted without discrimination related to the origin of the products concerned;

(b) aid to make good the damage caused by natural disasters or exceptional occurrences;

(c) aid granted to the economy of certain areas of the Federal Republic of Germany affected by the division of Germany, insofar as such aid is required in order to compensate for the economic disadvantages caused by that division.

3.   The following may be considered to be compatible with the internal market:

(a) aid to promote the economic development of areas where the standard of living is abnormally low or where there is serious underemployment;

(b) aid to promote the execution of an important project of common European interest or to remedy a serious disturbance in the economy of a Member State;

(c) aid to facilitate the development of certain economic activities or of certain economic areas, where such aid does not adversely affect trading conditions to an extent contrary to the common interest;

(d) aid to promote culture and heritage conservation where such aid does not affect trading conditions and competition in the Union to an extent that is contrary to the common interest;

(e) such other categories of aid as may be specified by European regulations or decisions adopted by the Council of Ministers on a proposal from the Commission.

Article III-57

1.   The Commission, in cooperation with Member States, shall keep under constant review all systems of aid existing in those States. It shall propose to the latter any appropriate measures required by the progressive development or by the functioning of the internal market.

2.   If, after giving notice to the parties concerned to submit their comments, the Commission finds that aid granted by a Member State or through State resources is not compatible with the internal market having regard to Article III-56, or that such aid is being misused, it shall adopt a European decision requiring the State concerned to abolish or alter such aid within a period of time to be determined by the Commission.

If the State concerned does not comply with this European decision within the prescribed time, the Commission or any other interested Member State may, in derogation from Articles III-265 and III-266, refer the matter to the Court of Justice direct.

On application by a Member State, the Council of Ministers may adopt unanimously a European decision that aid which that State is granting or intends to grant shall be considered to be compatible with the internal market, in derogation from Article III-56 or from European regulations provided for in Article III-58, if such a decision is justified by exceptional circumstances. If, as regards the aid in question, the Commission has already initiated the procedure provided for in the first subparagraph of this paragraph, the fact that the State concerned has made its application to the Council of Ministers shall have the effect of suspending that procedure until the Council of Ministers has made its attitude known.

If, however, the Council of Ministers has not made its attitude known within three months of the said application being made, the Commission shall act.

3.   The Commission shall be informed by the Member States, in sufficient time to enable it to submit its comments, of any plans to grant or alter aid. If it considers that any such plan is not compatible with the internal market having regard to Article III-56, it shall without delay initiate the procedure provided for in paragraph 2. The Member State concerned shall not put its proposed measures into effect until this procedure has resulted in a final decision.

4.   The Commission may adopt European regulations relating to the categories of State aid that the Council of Ministers has, pursuant to Article III-58, determined may be exempted from the procedure provided for by paragraph 3.

Article III-58

The Council of Ministers, on a proposal from the Commission, may adopt European regulations for the application of Articles III-56 and III-57 and for determining in particular the conditions in which Article III-57(3) shall apply and the categories of aid exempted from this procedure. It shall act after consulting the European Parliament.

Section 6   FISCAL PROVISIONS

Article III-59

No Member State shall impose, directly or indirectly, on the products of other Member States any internal taxation of any kind in excess of that imposed directly or indirectly on similar domestic products.

Furthermore, no Member State shall impose on the products of other Member States any internal taxation of such a nature as to afford indirect protection to other products.

Article III-60

Where products are exported by a Member State to the territory of another Member State, any repayment of internal taxation shall not exceed the internal taxation imposed on them whether directly or indirectly.

Article III-61

In the case of charges other than turnover taxes, excise duties and other forms of indirect taxation, remissions and repayments in respect of exports to other Member States may not be granted and countervailing charges in respect of imports from Member States may not be imposed unless the provisions contemplated have been previously approved for a limited period by a European decision adopted by the Council of Ministers on a proposal from the Commission.

Article III-62

1.   A European law or framework law of the Council of Ministers shall lay down measures for the harmonisation of legislation concerning turnover taxes, excise duties and other forms of indirect taxation provided that such harmonisation is necessary for the functioning of the internal market and to avoid distortion of competition. The Council of Ministers shall act unanimously after consulting the European Parliament and the Economic and Social Committee.

2.   Where the Council of Ministers, acting unanimously on a proposal from the Commission, finds that the measures referred to in paragraph 1 relate to administrative cooperation or to combating tax fraud and tax evasion, it shall act, notwithstanding paragraph 1, by a qualified majority when adopting the European law or framework law adopting these measures.

Article III-63

Where the Council of Ministers, acting unanimously on a proposal from the Commission, finds that measures on company taxation relate to administrative cooperation or combating tax fraud and tax evasion, it shall adopt, by a qualified majority, a European law or framework law laying down these measures, provided that they are necessary for the functioning of the internal market and to avoid distortion of competition.

That law or framework law shall be adopted after consultation of the European Parliament and the Economic and Social Committee.

Section 7   APPROXIMATION OF LEGISLATION

Article III-64

Without prejudice to Article III-65, a European framework law of the Council of Ministers shall establish measures for the approximation of such laws, regulations or administrative provisions of the Member States as directly affect the establishment or functioning of the internal market. The Council of Ministers shall act unanimously after consulting the European Parliament and the Economic and Social Committee.

Article III-65

1.　　　　Save where otherwise provided in the Constitution, this Article shall apply for the achievement of the objectives set out in Article III-14. European laws or framework laws shall establish measures for the approximation of the provisions laid down by law, regulation or administrative action in Member States which have as their object the establishment and functioning of the internal market. Such laws shall be adopted after consultation of the Economic and Social Committee.

2.　　　　Paragraph 1 shall not apply to fiscal provisions, to those relating to the free movement of persons or to those relating to the rights and interests of employed persons.

3.　　　　The Commission, in its proposals submitted under paragraph 1 concerning health, safety, environmental protection and consumer protection, will take as a base a high level of protection, taking account in particular of any new development based on scientific facts. Within their respective powers, the European Parliament and the Council of Ministers will also seek to achieve this objective.

4.　　　　If, after the adoption of a harmonisation measure by means of a European law, framework law or regulation of the Commission, a Member State deems it necessary to maintain national provisions on grounds of major needs referred to in Article III-43, or relating to the protection of the environment or the working environment, it shall notify the Commission of these provisions as well as the grounds for maintaining them.

5.　　　　Moreover, without prejudice to paragraph 4, if, after the adoption of a harmonisation measure by means of a European law, framework law or regulation of the Commission, a Member State deems it necessary to introduce national provisions based on new scientific evidence relating to the protection of the environment or the working environment on grounds of a problem specific to that Member State arising after the adoption of the harmonisation measure, it shall notify the Commission of the envisaged provisions and the reasons for them.

6.　　　　The Commission shall, within six months of the notifications referred to in paragraphs 4 and 5, adopt a European decision approving or rejecting the national provisions involved after having verified whether or not they are a means of arbitrary discrimination or a disguised restriction on trade between Member States and whether or not they constitute an obstacle to the functioning of the internal market.

In the absence of a decision by the Commission within this period the national provisions referred to in paragraphs 4 and 5 shall be deemed to have been approved.

When justified by the complexity of the matter and in the absence of danger for human health, the Commission may notify the Member State concerned that the period referred to in this paragraph may be extended for a further period of up to six months.

7.   When, pursuant to paragraph 6, a Member State is authorised to maintain or introduce national provisions derogating from a harmonisation measure, the Commission shall immediately examine whether to propose an adaptation to that measure.

8.   When a Member State raises a specific problem on public health in a field which has been the subject of prior harmonisation measures, it shall bring it to the attention of the Commission which shall immediately examine whether to propose appropriate measures.

9.   By way of derogation from the procedure laid down in Articles III-265 and III-266, the Commission and any Member State may bring the matter directly before the Court of Justice if it considers that another Member State is making improper use of the powers provided for in this Article.

10.   The harmonisation measures referred to in this Article shall, in appropriate cases, include a safeguard clause authorising the Member States to take, for one or more of the non-economic reasons referred to in Article III-43, provisional steps subject to a Union control procedure.

Article III-66

Where the Commission finds that a difference between the provisions laid down by law, regulation or administrative action in Member States is distorting the conditions of competition in the internal market and that the resultant distortion needs to be eliminated, it shall consult the Member States concerned.

If such consultation does not result in agreement, European framework laws shall eliminate the distortion in question. Any other appropriate measures provided for in the Constitution may be adopted.

Article III-67

1.   Where there is a reason to fear that the adoption or amendment of a national provision laid down by law, regulation or administrative action may cause distortion within the meaning of Article III-66, a Member State desiring to proceed therewith shall consult the Commission. After consulting the Member States, the Commission shall address to the Member States concerned a recommendation on such measures as may be appropriate to avoid the distortion in question.

2.   If a Member State desiring to introduce or amend its own provisions does not comply with the recommendation addressed to it by the Commission, other Member States shall not be required, pursuant to Article III-66, to amend their own provisions in order to eliminate such distortion. If the Member State which has ignored the recommendation of the Commission causes distortion detrimental only to itself, Article III-66 shall not apply.

Article III-68

In establishing an internal market, measures for the introduction of European instruments to provide uniform intellectual-property rights protection throughout the Union and for the setting up of centralised Union-wide authorisation, coordination and supervision arrangements shall be established in European laws or framework laws.

A European law of the Council of Ministers shall establish language arrangements for the European instruments. The Council of Ministers shall act unanimously after consulting the European Parliament.

Chapter II

ECONOMIC AND MONETARY POLICY

Article III-69

1.   For the purposes set out in Article I-3, the activities of the Member States and the Union shall include, as provided in the Constitution, the adoption of an economic policy which is based on the close coordination of Member States' economic policies, on the internal market and on the definition of common objectives, and conducted in accordance with the principle of an open market economy with free competition.

2.   Concurrently with the foregoing, and as provided in the Constitution and in accordance with the procedures set out therein, these activities shall include a single currency, the euro, and the definition and conduct of a single monetary policy and exchange-rate policy, the primary objective of both of which shall be to maintain price stability and, without prejudice to this objective, to support the general economic policies in the Union, in accordance with the principle of an open market economy with free competition.

3.   These activities of the Member States and the Union shall entail compliance with the following guiding principles: stable prices, sound public finances and monetary conditions and a stable balance of payments.

Section 1 ECONOMIC POLICY

Article III-70

Member States shall conduct their economic policies in order to contribute to the achievement of the Union's objectives, as defined in Article I-3, and in the context of the broad guidelines referred to in Article III-71(2). The Member States and the Union shall act in accordance with the principle of an open market economy with free competition, favouring an efficient allocation of resources, and in compliance with the principles set out in Article III-69.

1.   Member States shall regard their economic policies as a matter of common concern and shall coordinate them within the Council of Ministers, in accordance with Article III-70.

2.   The Council of Ministers, on a recommendation from the Commission, shall formulate a draft for the broad guidelines of the economic policies of the Member States and of the Union, and shall report its findings to the European Council.

The European Council, on the basis of the report from the Council of Ministers, shall discuss a conclusion on the broad guidelines of the economic policies of the Member States and of the Union. On the basis of this conclusion, the Council of Ministers shall adopt a recommendation setting out these broad guidelines. It shall inform the European Parliament of its recommendation.

3.   In order to ensure closer coordination of economic policies and sustained convergence of the economic performances of the Member States, the Council of Ministers, on the basis of reports submitted by the Commission, shall monitor economic developments in each of the Member States and in the Union, as well as the consistency of economic policies with the broad guidelines referred to in paragraph 2, and shall regularly carry out an overall assessment.

For the purpose of this multilateral surveillance, Member States shall forward information to the Commission on important steps taken by them in the field of their economic policy and such other information as they deem necessary.

4.   Where it is established, under the procedure referred to in paragraph 3, that the economic policies of a Member State are not consistent with the broad guidelines referred to in paragraph 2 or that they risk jeopardising the proper functioning of economic and monetary union, the Commission may address a warning to the Member State concerned. The Council of Ministers, on a recommendation from the Commission, may address the necessary recommendations to the Member State concerned. The Council of Ministers, on a proposal from the Commission, may decide to make its recommendations public.

Within the scope of this paragraph, the Council of Ministers shall act without taking into account the vote of the representative of the Member State concerned, and a qualified majority shall be defined as the majority of the votes of the other Member States, representing at least three fifths of their population.

5.   The President of the Council of Ministers and the Commission shall report to the European Parliament on the results of multilateral surveillance. The President of the Council of Ministers may be invited to appear before the competent committee of the European Parliament if the Council of Ministers has made its recommendations public.

6.   European laws may lay down detailed rules for the multilateral surveillance procedure referred to in paragraphs 3 and 4.

Article III-72

1.   Without prejudice to any other procedures provided for by the Constitution, the Council of Ministers, on a proposal from the Commission, may adopt a European decision laying down the measures appropriate to the economic situation, in particular if severe difficulties arise in the supply of certain products.

2.   Where a Member State is in difficulties or is seriously threatened with severe difficulties caused by natural disasters or exceptional occurrences beyond its control, the Council of Ministers, on a proposal from the Commission, may adopt a European decision granting, under certain conditions, Union financial assistance to the Member State concerned. The President of the Council of Ministers shall inform the European Parliament of the decision adopted.

Article III-73

1.   Overdraft facilities or any other type of credit facility with the European Central Bank or with the central banks of the Member States (hereinafter referred to as "national central banks") in favour of Union institutions, bodies or agencies, central governments, regional, local or other public authorities, other bodies governed by public law, or public undertakings of Member States shall be prohibited, as shall the purchase directly from them by the European Central Bank or national central banks of debt instruments.

2.   Paragraph 1 shall not apply to publicly owned credit institutions which, in the context of the supply of reserves by central banks, shall be given the same treatment by national central banks and the European Central Bank as private credit institutions.

Article III-74

1.   Any measure or provision, not based on prudential considerations, establishing privileged access by Union institutions, bodies or agencies, central governments, regional, local or other public authorities, other bodies governed by public law, or public undertakings of Member States to financial institutions shall be prohibited.

2.   The Council of Ministers, on a proposal from the Commission, may adopt European regulations or decisions specifying definitions for the application of the prohibition referred to in paragraph 1. It shall act after consulting the European Parliament.

Article III-75

1.   The Union shall not be liable for or assume the commitments of central governments, regional, local or other public authorities, other bodies governed by public law, or public undertakings of any Member State, without prejudice to mutual financial guarantees for the joint execution of a specific project. A Member State shall not be liable for or assume the commitments of central governments, regional, local or other public authorities, other bodies governed by public law, or public undertakings of another Member State, without prejudice to mutual financial guarantees for the joint execution of a specific project.

2.   The Council of Ministers, on a proposal from the Commission, may adopt European regulations or decisions specifying definitions for the application of the prohibitions referred to in Article III-73 and in this Article. It shall act after consulting the European Parliament.

Article III-76

1.　　　　Member States shall avoid excessive government deficits.

2.　　　　The Commission shall monitor the development of the budgetary situation and of the stock of government debt in the Member States in order to identify gross errors. In particular it shall examine compliance with budgetary discipline on the basis of the following two criteria:

(a) whether the ratio of the planned or actual government deficit to gross domestic product exceeds a reference value, unless:

(i) either the ratio has declined substantially and continuously and reached a level that comes close to the reference value;
(ii) or, alternatively, the excess over the reference value is only exceptional and temporary and the ratio remains close to the reference value;

(b) whether the ratio of government debt to gross domestic product exceeds a reference value, unless the ratio is diminishing sufficiently and approaching the reference value at a satisfactory pace.

The reference values are specified in the Protocol on the excessive deficit procedure.

3.　　　　If a Member State does not fulfil the requirements under one or both of these criteria, the Commission shall prepare a report. The report of the Commission shall also take into account whether the government deficit exceeds government investment expenditure and take into account all other relevant factors, including the medium-term economic and budgetary position of the Member State.

The Commission may also prepare a report if, notwithstanding the fulfilment of the requirements under the criteria, it is of the opinion that there is a risk of an excessive deficit in a Member State.

4.　　　　The Economic and Financial Committee shall formulate an opinion on the report of the Commission.

5.   If the Commission considers that an excessive deficit in a Member State exists or may occur, it shall address an opinion to the Member State concerned.

6.   The Council of Ministers shall, on a proposal from the Commission, having considered any observations which the Member State concerned may wish to make and after an overall assessment, decide whether an excessive deficit exists. In that case it shall adopt, according to the same procedures, recommendations addressed to the Member State concerned with a view to bringing that situation to an end within a given period. Subject to paragraph 8, those recommendations shall not be made public.

Within the scope of this paragraph, the Council of Ministers shall act without taking into account the vote of the representative of the Member State concerned, and a qualified majority shall be defined as the majority of the votes of the other Member States, representing at least three fifths of their population.

7.   The Council of Ministers, on a recommendation from the Commission, shall adopt the European decisions and recommendations referred to in paragraphs 8 to 11. It shall act without taking into account the vote of the representative of the Member State concerned, and a qualified majority shall be defined as the majority of the other Member States, representing at least three fifths of their population.

8.   Where it establishes that there has been no effective action in response to its recommendations within the period laid down, the Council of Ministers may make its recommendations public.

9.   If a Member State persists in failing to put into practice the recommendations of the Council of Ministers, the Council of Ministers may adopt a European decision giving notice to the Member State to take, within a specified time-limit, steps for the deficit reduction which is judged necessary by the Council of Ministers in order to remedy the situation.

In such a case, the Council of Ministers may request the Member State concerned to submit reports in accordance with a specific timetable in order to examine the adjustment efforts of that Member State.

10.   As long as a Member State fails to comply with a European decision adopted in accordance with paragraph 9, the Council of Ministers may decide to apply or, as the case may be, intensify one or more of the following measures:

(a) to require the Member State concerned to publish additional information, to be specified by the Council of Ministers, before issuing bonds and securities;

(b) to invite the European Investment Bank to reconsider its lending policy towards the Member State concerned;

(c) to require the Member State concerned to make a non-interest-bearing deposit of an appropriate size with the Union until the Council of Ministers considers that the excessive deficit has been corrected;

(d) to impose fines of an appropriate size.

The President of the Council of Ministers shall inform the European Parliament of the measures adopted.

11. The Council of Ministers shall abrogate some or all of the measures referred to in paragraph 6 and paragraphs 8 to 10 if it considers the excessive deficit in the Member State concerned to have been corrected. If the Council of Ministers has previously made public recommendations, it shall state publicly, as soon as the decision under paragraph 8 has been abrogated, that there is no longer an excessive deficit in the Member State concerned.

12. The rights to bring actions provided for in Articles III-265 and III-266 may not be exercised within the framework of paragraphs 1 to 6 or paragraphs 8 and 9.

13. Further provisions relating to the implementation of the procedure described in this Article are set out in the Protocol on the excessive deficit procedure.

A European law of the Council of Ministers shall lay down the appropriate measures to replace the said Protocol. The Council of Ministers shall act unanimously after consulting the European Parliament and the European Central Bank.

Subject to the other provisions of this paragraph, the Council of Ministers, on a proposal from the Commission, shall adopt European regulations or decisions laying down detailed rules and definitions for the application of the said Protocol. It shall act after consulting the European Parliament.

MONETARY POLICY

Article III-77

1.   The primary objective of the European System of Central Banks shall be to maintain price stability. Without prejudice to this objective, the European System of Central Banks shall support the general economic policies in the Union in order to contribute to the achievement of its objectives as laid down in Article I-3. The European System of Central Banks shall act in accordance with the principle of an open market economy with free competition, favouring an efficient allocation of resources, and in compliance with the principles set out in Article III-69.

2.   The basic tasks to be carried out through the European System of Central Banks shall be:

> (a) to define and implement the Union's monetary policy;
> (b) to conduct foreign-exchange operations consistent with Article III-228;
> (c) to hold and manage the official foreign reserves of the Member States;
> (d) to promote the smooth operation of payment systems.

3.   Paragraph 2(c) shall be without prejudice to the holding and management by the governments of Member States of foreign-exchange working balances.

4.   The European Central Bank shall be consulted:

> (a) on any proposed Union act in its fields of competence;
> (b) by national authorities regarding any draft legislative provision in its fields of competence, but within the limits and under the conditions set out by the Council of Ministers in accordance with the procedure laid down in Article III-79(6).

The European Central Bank may submit opinions to the Union institutions, bodies or agencies or to national authorities on matters in its fields of competence.

5.   The European System of Central Banks shall contribute to the smooth conduct of policies pursued by the competent authorities relating to the prudential supervision of credit institutions and the stability of the financial system.

6.　　　　European laws may confer upon the European Central Bank specific tasks concerning policies relating to the prudential supervision of credit institutions and other financial institutions with the exception of insurance undertakings. Such laws shall be adopted after consultation of the European Central Bank.

Article III-78

1.　　　　The European Central Bank shall have the exclusive right to authorise the issue of euro bank notes in the Union. The European Central Bank and the national central banks may issue such notes. Only the bank notes issued by the European Central Bank and the national central banks shall have the status of legal tender within the Union.

2.　　　　Member States may issue euro coins subject to approval by the European Central Bank of the volume of the issue. The Council of Ministers, on a proposal from the Commission, may adopt European regulations laying down measures to harmonise the denominations and technical specifications of all coins intended for circulation to the extent necessary to permit their smooth circulation within the Union. The Council of Ministers shall act after consulting the European Parliament and the European Central Bank.

Article III-79

1.　　　　The European System of Central Banks shall be composed of the European Central Bank and of the national central banks.

2.　　　　The European Central Bank shall have legal personality.

3.　　　　The European System of Central Banks shall be governed by the decision-making bodies of the European Central Bank, which shall be the Governing Council and the Executive Board.

4.　　　　The Statute of the European System of Central Banks is laid down in the Protocol on the Statute of the European System of Central Banks and the European Central Bank.

5.　　　　Articles 5.1, 5.2, 5.3, 17, 18, 19.1, 22, 23, 24, 26, 32.2, 32.3, 32.4, 32.6, 33.1(a) and 36 of the Statute of the European System of Central Banks and the European Central Bank may be amended by European laws:

> (a) either on a proposal from the Commission after consultation of the European Central Bank;
>
> (b) or on a recommendation from the European Central Bank after consultation of the Commission.

6.　　　　The Council of Ministers shall adopt the European regulations and decisions laying down the measures referred to in Articles 4, 5.4, 19.2, 20, 28.1, 29.2, 30.4 and 34.3 of the Statute of the System of European Central Banks and the European Central Bank. It shall act after consulting the European Parliament:

> (a) either on a proposal from the Commission after consulting the European Central Bank;
>
> (b) or on a recommendation from the European Central Bank after consulting the Commission.

Article III-80

When exercising the powers and carrying out the tasks and duties conferred upon them by the Constitution and the Statute of the European System of Central Banks and the European Central Bank, neither the European Central Bank, nor a national central bank, nor any member of their decision-making bodies shall seek or take instructions from Union institutions, bodies or agencies, from any government of a Member State or from any other body. The Union institutions, bodies or agencies and the governments of the Member States undertake to respect this principle and not to seek to influence the members of the decision-making bodies of the European Central Bank or of the national central banks in the performance of their tasks.

Article III-81

Each Member State shall ensure that its national legislation, including the statutes of its national central bank, is compatible with the Constitution and the Statute of the European System of Central Banks and the European Central Bank.

Article III-82

1.   In order to carry out the tasks entrusted to the European System of Central Banks, the European Central Bank shall, in accordance with the Constitution and under the conditions laid down in the Statute of the European System of Central Banks and the European Central Bank, adopt:

> (a) European regulations to the extent necessary to implement the tasks defined in Article 3.1, first indent, Articles 19.1, 22 and 25.2 of the Statute of the European System of Central Banks and the European Central Bank and in cases which shall be laid down in European regulations and decisions as referred to in Article III-79(6);
> (b) European decisions necessary for carrying out the tasks entrusted to the European System of Central Banks under the Constitution and the Statute of the European System of Central Banks and the European Central Bank;
> (c) recommendations and opinions.

2.   The European Central Bank may decide to publish its European decisions, recommendations and opinions.

3.   The Council of Ministers shall, under the procedure laid down in Article III-79(6), adopt the European regulations establishing the limits and conditions under which the European Central Bank shall be entitled to impose fines or periodic penalty payments on undertakings for failure to comply with obligations under its European regulations and decisions.

Article III-83

Without prejudice to the powers of the European Central Bank, a European law or framework law shall lay down the measures necessary for use of the euro as the single currency of the Member States. Such law or framework law shall be adopted after consultation of the European Central Bank.

INSTITUTIONAL PROVISIONS

Article III-84

1.   The Governing Council of the European Central Bank shall comprise the members of the Executive Board of the European Central Bank and the Governors of the national central banks of the Member States without a derogation as referred to in Article III-91.

2.   (a) The Executive Board shall comprise the President, the Vice-President and four other members.

(b) The President, the Vice-President and the other members of the Executive Board shall be appointed from among persons of recognised standing and professional experience in monetary or banking matters by common accord of the governments of the Member States at the level of Heads of State or Government, on a recommendation from the Council of Ministers, after it has consulted the European Parliament and the Governing Council of the European Central Bank.

Their term of office shall be eight years and shall not be renewable.

Only nationals of Member States may be members of the Executive Board.

Article III-85

1.   The President of the Council of Ministers and a member of the Commission may participate, without having the right to vote, in meetings of the Governing Council of the European Central Bank.

The President of the Council of Ministers may submit a motion for deliberation to the Governing Council of the European Central Bank.

2.   The President of the European Central Bank shall be invited to participate in meetings of the Council of Ministers when it is discussing matters relating to the objectives and tasks of the European System of Central Banks.

3.   The European Central Bank shall address an annual report on the activities of the European System of Central Banks and on the monetary policy of both the previous and the current year to the European Parliament, the Council of Ministers and the Commission, and also to the European Council. The President of the European Central Bank shall present this report to the Council of Ministers and to the European Parliament, which may hold a general debate on that basis.

The President of the European Central Bank and the other members of the Executive Board may, at the request of the European Parliament or on their own initiative, be heard by the competent committees of the European Parliament.

Article III-86

1.   In order to promote coordination of the policies of Member States to the full extent needed for the functioning of the internal market, an Economic and Financial Committee is hereby set up.

2.   The Committee shall have the following tasks:

(a) to deliver opinions at the request of the Council of Ministers or of the Commission, or on its own initiative, for submission to those institutions;

(b) to keep under review the economic and financial situation of the Member States and of the Union and to report on it regularly to the Council of Ministers and to the Commission, in particular with regard to financial relations with third countries and international institutions;

(c) without prejudice to Article III-247, to contribute to the preparation of the work of the Council of Ministers referred to in Article III-48, Article III-71(2), (3), (4) and (6), Articles III-72, III-74, III-75 and III-76, Article III-77(6), Article III-78(2), Article III-79(5) and (6), Articles III-83 and III-90, Article III-92(2) and (3), Article III-95, Article III-96(2) and (3) and Articles III-224 and III-228, and to carry out other advisory and preparatory tasks assigned to it by the Council of Ministers;

(d) to examine, at least once a year, the situation regarding the movement of capital and the freedom of payments, as they result from the application of the Constitution and of Union acts; the examination shall cover all measures relating to capital movements and payments; the Committee shall report to the Commission and to the Council of Ministers on the outcome of this examination.

The Member States, the Commission and the European Central Bank shall each appoint no more than two members of the Committee.

3.   The Council of Ministers, on a proposal from the Commission, shall adopt a European decision laying down detailed provisions concerning the composition of the Economic and Financial Committee. It shall act after consulting the European Central Bank and the Committee. The President of the Council of Ministers shall inform the European Parliament of that decision.

4.   In addition to the tasks set out in paragraph 2, if and as long as there are Member States with a derogation as referred to in Article III-91, the Committee shall keep under review the monetary and financial situation and the general payments system of those Member States and report regularly to the Council of Ministers and to the Commission on the matter.

Article III-87

For matters within the scope of Article III-71(4), Article III-76 with the exception of paragraph 13, Articles III-83, III-90 and III-91, Article III-92(3) and Article III-228, the Council of Ministers or a Member State may request the Commission to make a recommendation or a proposal, as appropriate. The Commission shall examine this request and submit its conclusions to the Council of Ministers without delay.

Section 3a   PROVISIONS SPECIFIC TO MEMBER STATES
WHICH ARE PART OF THE EURO AREA

Article III-88

1.   In order to ensure that economic and monetary union works properly, and in accordance with the relevant provisions of the Constitution, measures specific to those Member States which are members of the euro area shall be adopted:

> (a) to strengthen the coordination of their budgetary discipline and surveillance of it;
> (b) to set out economic policy guidelines for them, while ensuring that they are compatible with those adopted for the whole of the Union and are kept under surveillance.

2.　　　　　　For those measures set out in paragraph 1, only members of the Council of Ministers representing Member States which are part of the euro area shall vote. A qualified majority shall be defined as the majority of the votes of the representatives of the Member States which are part of the euro area, representing at least three fifths of their population. Unanimity of those members of the Council of Ministers shall be required for an act requiring unanimity.

Article III-89

Arrangements for meetings between ministers of those Member States which are part of the euro area shall be laid down in the Protocol on the Euro Group.

Article III-90

1.　　　　　　In order to secure the euro's place in the international monetary system, the Council of Ministers, on a proposal from the Commission and after consulting the European Central Bank, shall adopt a European decision establishing common positions on matters of particular interest for economic and monetary union within the competent international financial institutions and conferences.

2.　　　　　　For the measures referred to in paragraph 1, only members of the Council of Ministers representing Member States which are part of the euro area shall vote. A qualified majority shall be defined as the majority of the votes of the representatives of the Member States which are part of the euro area, representing at least three fifths of their population. Unanimity of those members of the Council of Ministers shall be required for an act requiring unanimity.

3.　　　　　　The Council of Ministers, on a proposal from the Commission, may adopt appropriate measures to ensure unified representation within the international financial institutions and conferences. The procedural provisions of paragraphs 1 and 2 shall apply.

TRANSITIONAL PROVISIONS

Article III-91

1.   Member States which the Council of Ministers has decided do not fulfil the necessary conditions for the adoption of the euro shall hereinafter be referred to as "Member States with a derogation".

2.   The following provisions of the Constitution shall not apply to Member States with a derogation:

> (a) adoption of the parts of the broad economic-policy guidelines which concern the euro area generally (Article III-71(2));
> (b) coercive means of remedying excessive deficits (Article III-76(9) and (10));
> (c) the objectives and tasks of the European System of Central Banks (Article III-77(1), (2), (3) and (5));
> (d) issue of the euro (Article III-78);
> (e) acts of the European Central Bank (Article III-82);
> (f) measures governing the use of the euro (Article III-83);
> (g) monetary agreements and other measures relating to exchange-rate policy (Article III-228);
> (h) appointment of members of the Executive Board of the European Central Bank (Article III-84(2)(b)).

In the Articles referred to above, "Member States" shall therefore mean Member States without a derogation.

3.   Under Chapter IX of the Statute of the European System of Central Banks and the European Central Bank, Member States with a derogation and their national central banks are excluded from rights and obligations within the European System of Central Banks.

4.   The voting rights of members of the Council of Ministers representing Member States with a derogation shall be suspended for the adoption by the Council of Ministers of the measures referred to in the Articles listed in paragraph 2. A qualified majority shall be defined as a majority of the votes of the representatives of the Member

States without a derogation, representing at least three fifths of their population. Unanimity of those Member States shall be required for any act requiring unanimity.

Article III-92

1.　　　　At least once every two years, or at the request of a Member State with a derogation, the Commission and the European Central Bank shall report to the Council of Ministers on the progress made by the Member States with a derogation in fulfilling their obligations regarding the achievement of economic and monetary union. These reports shall include an examination of the compatibility between each of these Member States' national legislation, including the statutes of its national central bank, and Articles III-80 and III-81 and the Statute of the European System of Central Banks and the European Central Bank. The reports shall also examine whether a high degree of sustainable convergence has been achieved, by analysing how far each of these Member States has fulfilled the following criteria:

(a) the achievement of a high degree of price stability; this will be apparent from a rate of inflation which is close to that of, at most, the three best performing Member States in terms of price stability;

(b) the sustainability of the government financial position; this will be apparent from having achieved a government budgetary position without a deficit that is excessive as determined in accordance with Article III-76(6);

(c) the observance of the normal fluctuation margins provided for by the exchange-rate mechanism for at least two years, without devaluing against the euro;

(d) the durability of convergence achieved by the Member State with a derogation and of its participation in the exchange-rate mechanism, being reflected in the long-term interest-rate levels.

The four criteria mentioned in this paragraph and the relevant periods over which they are to be respected are developed further in the Protocol on the convergence criteria. The reports of the Commission and the European Central Bank shall also take account of the results of the integration of markets, the situation and development of the balances of payments on current account and an examination of the development of unit labour costs and other price indices.

2.   After consulting the European Parliament and after discussion in the European Council, the Council of Ministers, on a proposal from the Commission, shall adopt a European decision establishing which Member States with a derogation fulfil the necessary conditions on the basis of the criteria set out in paragraph 1, and shall abrogate the derogations of the Member States concerned.

3.   If it is decided, according to the procedure set out in paragraph 2, to abrogate a derogation, the Council of Ministers shall, on a proposal from the Commission, with the unanimity of the members representing Member States without a derogation and the Member State concerned, adopt the European regulations or decisions irrevocably fixing the rate at which the euro is to be substituted for the currency of the Member State concerned, and laying down the other measures necessary for the introduction of the euro as the single currency in that Member State. The Council of Ministers shall act after consulting the European Central Bank.

Article III-93

1.   If and as long as there are Member States with a derogation, and without prejudice to Article III-79(3), the General Council of the European Central Bank referred to in Article 45 of the Statute of the European System of Central Banks and the European Central Bank shall be constituted as a third decision-making body of the European Central Bank.

2.   If and as long as there are Member States with a derogation, the European Central Bank shall, as regards those Member States:

(a) strengthen cooperation between the national central banks;
(b) strengthen the coordination of the monetary policies of the Member States, with the aim of ensuring price stability;
(c) monitor the functioning of the exchange-rate mechanism;
(d) hold consultations concerning issues falling within the competence of the national central banks and affecting the stability of financial institutions and markets;
(e) carry out the former tasks of the European Monetary Cooperation Fund, previously taken over by the European Monetary Institute.

Article III-94

Each Member State with a derogation shall treat its exchange-rate policy as a matter of common interest. In so doing, it shall take account of the experience acquired in cooperation within the framework of the exchange-rate mechanism.

Article III-95

1.   Where a Member State with a derogation is in difficulties or is seriously threatened with difficulties as regards its balance of payments either as a result of an overall disequilibrium in its balance of payments, or as a result of the type of currency at its disposal, and where such difficulties are liable in particular to jeopardise the functioning of the internal market or the implementation of the common commercial policy, the Commission shall immediately investigate the position of the State in question and the action which, making use of all the means at its disposal, that State has taken or may take in accordance with the Constitution. The Commission shall state what measures it recommends the Member State concerned to adopt.

If the action taken by a Member State with a derogation and the measures suggested by the Commission do not prove sufficient to overcome the difficulties which have arisen or which threaten, the Commission shall, after consulting the Economic and Financial Committee, recommend to the Council of Ministers the granting of mutual assistance and appropriate methods.

The Commission shall keep the Council of Ministers regularly informed of the situation and of how it evolves.

2.   The Council of Ministers shall grant such mutual assistance; it shall adopt European regulations or decisions laying down the conditions and details of such assistance, which may take such forms as:

    (a) a concerted approach to or within any other international organisations to which Member States with a derogation may have recourse;

    (b) measures needed to avoid deflection of trade where the Member State with a derogation which is in difficulties maintains or reintroduces quantitative restrictions against third countries;

    (c) the granting of limited credits by other Member States, subject to their agreement.

3. If the mutual assistance recommended by the Commission is not granted by the Council of Ministers or if the mutual assistance granted and the measures taken are insufficient, the Commission shall authorise the Member State with a derogation which is in difficulties to take protective measures, the conditions and details of which the Commission shall determine.

Such authorisation may be revoked and such conditions and details may be changed by the Council of Ministers.

Article III-96

1. Where a sudden crisis in the balance of payments occurs and an act within the meaning of Article III-95(2) is not immediately adopted, a Member State with a derogation may, as a precaution, take the necessary protective measures. Such measures must cause the least possible disturbance in the functioning of the internal market and must not be wider in scope than is strictly necessary to remedy the sudden difficulties which have arisen.

2. The Commission and the other Member States shall be informed of such protective measures not later than when they enter into force. The Commission may recommend to the Council of Ministers the granting of mutual assistance under Article III-95.

3. After the Commission has delivered an opinion and the Economic and Financial Committee has been consulted, the Council of Ministers may adopt a decision stipulating that the Member State concerned shall amend, suspend or abolish the protective measures referred to above.

Chapter III POLICIES IN OTHER SPECIFIC AREAS

Section 1 EMPLOYMENT

Article III-97

The Union and the Member States shall, in accordance with this Section, work towards developing a coordinated strategy for employment and particularly for promoting a skilled, trained and adaptable workforce and labour markets responsive to economic change with a view to achieving the objectives defined in Article I-3.

Article III-98

1.   Member States, through their employment policies, shall contribute to the achievement of the objectives referred to in Article III-97 in a way consistent with the broad guidelines of the economic policies of the Member States and of the Union adopted pursuant to Article III-71(2).

2.   Member States, having regard to national practices related to the responsibilities of the social partners, shall regard promoting employment as a matter of common concern and shall coordinate their action in this respect within the Council of Ministers, in accordance with Article III-100.

Article III-99

1.   The Union shall contribute to a high level of employment by encouraging cooperation between Member States and by supporting and, if necessary, complementing their action. In doing so, the competences of the Member States shall be respected.

2.   The objective of a high level of employment shall be taken into consideration in the formulation and implementation of Union policies and activities.

Article III-100

1.   The European Council shall each year consider the employment situation in the Union and adopt conclusions thereon, on the basis of a joint annual report by the Council of Ministers and the Commission.

2.   On the basis of the conclusions of the European Council, the Council of Ministers, on a proposal from the Commission, shall each year adopt guidelines which the Member States shall take into account in their employment policies. It shall act after consulting the European Parliament, the Committee of the Regions, the Economic and Social Committee and the Employment Committee.

These guidelines shall be consistent with the broad guidelines adopted pursuant to Article III-71(2).

3.   Each Member State shall provide the Council of Ministers and the Commission with an annual report on the principal steps taken to implement its employment policy in the light of the guidelines for employment as referred to in paragraph 2.

4.   The Council of Ministers, on the basis of the reports referred to in paragraph 3 and having received the views of the Employment Committee, shall each year carry out an examination of the implementation of the employment policies of the Member States in the light of the guidelines for employment. The Council of Ministers, on a recommendation from the Commission, may adopt recommendations which it shall address to Member States.

5.   On the basis of the results of that examination, the Council of Ministers and the Commission shall make a joint annual report to the European Council on the employment situation in the Union and on the implementation of the guidelines for employment.

Article III-101

European laws or framework laws may establish incentive measures designed to encourage cooperation between Member States and to support their action in the field of employment through initiatives aimed at developing exchanges of information and best practices, providing comparative analysis and advice as well as promoting innovative approaches and evaluating experiences, in particular by recourse to pilot projects. They shall be adopted after consultation with the Committee of the Regions and the Economic and Social Committee.

Such European laws or framework laws shall not include harmonisation of the laws and regulations of the Member States.

Article III-102

The Council of Ministers shall, by simple majority, adopt a European decision establishing an Employment Committee with advisory status to promote coordination between Member States on employment and labour market policies. It shall act after consulting the European Parliament.

The tasks of the Committee shall be:

> (a) to monitor the employment situation and employment policies in the Member States and the Union;
> (b) without prejudice to Article III-247, to formulate opinions at the request of either the Council of Ministers or the Commission or on its own initiative, and to contribute to the preparation of the Council of Ministers proceedings referred to in Article III-100.

In fulfilling its mandate, the Committee shall consult the social partners.

Each Member State and the Commission shall appoint two members of the Committee.

Section 2 SOCIAL POLICY

Article III-103

The Union and the Member States, having in mind fundamental social rights such as those set out in the European Social Charter signed at Turin on 18 October 1961 and in the 1989 Community Charter of the Fundamental Social Rights of Workers, shall have as their objectives the promotion of employment, improved living and working conditions, so as to make possible their harmonisation while the improvement is being maintained, proper social protection, dialogue between the social partners, the development of human resources with a view to lasting high employment and the combating of exclusion.

To this end the Union and the Member States shall act taking account of the diverse forms of national practices, in particular in the field of contractual relations, and the need to maintain the competitiveness of the Union economy.

They believe that such a development will ensue not only from the functioning of the internal market, which will favour the harmonisation of social systems, but also from the procedures provided for in the Constitution and from the approximation of provisions laid down by law, regulation or administrative action.

Article III-104

1.   With a view to achieving the objectives of Article III-103, the Union shall support and complement the activities of the Member States in the following fields:

(a) improvement in particular of the working environment to protect workers' health and safety;

(b) working conditions;

(c) social security and social protection of workers;

(d) protection of workers where their employment contract is terminated;

(e) the information and consultation of workers;

(f) representation and collective defence of the interests of workers and employers, including co-determination, subject to paragraph 6;

(g) conditions of employment for third-country nationals legally residing in Union territory;

(h) the integration of persons excluded from the labour market, without prejudice to Article III-183;

(i) equality between men and women with regard to labour market opportunities and treatment at work;

(j) the combating of social exclusion;

(k) the modernisation of social protection systems without prejudice to point (c).

2.		To this end:

    (a) European laws or framework laws may establish measures designed to encourage cooperation between Member States through initiatives aimed at improving knowledge, developing exchanges of information and best practices, promoting innovative approaches and evaluating experiences, excluding any harmonisation of the laws and regulations of the Member States;

    (b) in the fields referred to in paragraph 1(a) to (i), European framework laws may establish minimum requirements for gradual implementation, having regard to the conditions and technical rules obtaining in each of the Member States. Such European framework laws shall avoid imposing administrative, financial and legal constraints in a way which would hold back the creation and development of small and medium-sized undertakings.

In all cases, such European laws or framework laws shall be adopted after consultation of the Committee of the Regions and the Economic and Social Committee.

3.		By way of derogation from paragraph 2, in the fields referred to in paragraph 1(c), (d), (f) and (g), European laws or framework laws shall be adopted by the Council of Ministers acting unanimously after consulting the European Parliament, the Committee of the Regions and the Economic and Social Committee.

The Council of Ministers may, on a proposal from the Commission, adopt a European decision making the ordinary legislative procedure applicable to paragraph 1(d), (f) and (g). It shall act unanimously after consulting the European Parliament.

4.		A Member State may entrust the social partners, at their joint request, with the implementation of European framework laws adopted pursuant to paragraph 2.

In this case, it shall ensure that, no later than the date on which a European framework law must be transposed, the social partners have introduced the necessary measures by agreement, the Member State concerned being required to take any necessary step enabling it at any time to be in a position to guarantee the results imposed by that framework law.

5.	The European laws and framework laws adopted pursuant to this Article:

(a) shall not affect the right of Member States to define the fundamental principles of their social security systems and must not significantly affect the financial equilibrium thereof;

(b) shall not prevent any Member State from maintaining or introducing more stringent protective measures compatible with the Constitution.

6.	This Article shall not apply to pay, the right of association, the right to strike or the right to impose lock-outs.

Article III-105

1.	The Commission shall have the task of promoting the consultation of the social partners at Union level and shall adopt any relevant measure to facilitate their dialogue by ensuring balanced support for the parties.

2.	To this end, before submitting proposals in the social policy field, the Commission shall consult the social partners on the possible direction of Union action.

3.	If, after such consultation, the Commission considers Union action desirable, it shall consult the social partners on the content of the envisaged proposal. The social partners shall forward to the Commission an opinion or, where appropriate, a recommendation.

4.	On the occasion of such consultation, the social partners may inform the Commission of their wish to initiate the process provided for in Article III-106. The duration of the procedure shall not exceed nine months, unless the social partners concerned and the Commission decide jointly to extend it.

Article III-106

1.	Should the social partners so desire, the dialogue between them at Union level may lead to contractual relations, including agreements.

2.   Agreements concluded at Union level shall be implemented either in accordance with the procedures and practices specific to the social partners and the Member States or, in matters covered by Article III-104, at the joint request of the signatory parties, by European regulations or decisions adopted by the Council of Ministers on a proposal from the Commission. The European Parliament shall be informed.

Where the agreement in question contains one or more provisions relating to one of the areas for which unanimity is required by virtue of Article III-104(3), the Council of Ministers shall act unanimously.

Article III-107

With a view to achieving the objectives of Article III-103 and without prejudice to the other provisions of the Constitution, the Commission shall encourage cooperation between the Member States and facilitate the coordination of their action in all social policy fields under this Section, particularly in matters relating to:

(a) employment;

(b) labour law and working conditions;

(c) basic and advanced vocational training;

(d) social security;

(e) prevention of occupational accidents and diseases;

(f) occupational hygiene;

(g) the right of association and collective bargaining between employers and workers.

To this end, the Commission shall act in close contact with Member States by making studies, delivering opinions and arranging consultations both on problems arising at national level and on those of concern to international organisations, in particular initiatives aiming at the establishment of guidelines and indicators, the organisation of exchange of best practice, and the preparation of the necessary elements for periodic monitoring and evaluation. The European Parliament shall be kept fully informed.

Before delivering the opinions provided for in this Article, the Commission shall consult the Economic and Social Committee.

Article III-108

1.   Each Member State shall ensure that the principle of equal pay for male and female workers for equal work or work of equal value is applied.

2.   For the purpose of this Article, "pay" means the ordinary basic or minimum wage or salary and any other consideration, whether in cash or in kind, which the worker receives directly or indirectly, in respect of his employment, from his employer.

Equal pay without discrimination based on sex means:

> (a) that pay for the same work at piece rates shall be calculated on the basis of the same unit of measurement;
> (b) that pay for work at time rates shall be the same for the same job.

3.   European laws or framework laws shall establish measures to ensure the application of the principle of equal opportunities and equal treatment of men and women in matters of employment and occupation, including the principle of equal pay for equal work or work of equal value. They shall be adopted after consultation of the Economic and Social Committee.

4.   With a view to ensuring full equality in practice between men and women in working life, the principle of equal treatment shall not prevent any Member State from maintaining or adopting measures providing for specific advantages in order to make it easier for the under-represented sex to pursue a vocational activity or to prevent or compensate for disadvantages in professional careers.

Article III-109

Member States shall endeavour to maintain the existing equivalence between paid holiday schemes.

Article III-110

The Commission shall draw up a report each year on progress in achieving the objectives of Article III-103, including the demographic situation in the Union. It shall forward the report to the European Parliament, the Council of Ministers and the Economic and Social Committee.

Article III-111

The Council of Ministers shall, by a simple majority, adopt a European decision establishing a Social Protection Committee with advisory status to promote cooperation on social protection policies between Member States and with the Commission. The Council of Ministers shall act after consulting the European Parliament.

The tasks of the Committee shall be:

      (a) to monitor the social situation and the development of social protection policies in the Member States and the Union;

      (b) to promote exchanges of information, experience and good practice between Member States and with the Commission;

      (c) without prejudice to Article III-247, to prepare reports, formulate opinions or undertake other work within its fields of competence, at the request of either the Council of Ministers or the Commission or on its own initiative.

In fulfilling its mandate, the Committee shall establish appropriate contacts with the social partners.

Each Member State and the Commission shall appoint two members of the Committee.

Article III-112

The Commission shall include a separate chapter on social developments within the Union in its annual report to the European Parliament.

The European Parliament may invite the Commission to draw up reports on any particular problems concerning social conditions.

Article III-113

In order to improve employment opportunities for workers in the internal market and to contribute thereby to raising the standard of living, a European Social Fund is hereby established; it shall aim to render the employment of workers easier and to increase their geographical and occupational mobility within the Union, and to facilitate their adaptation to industrial changes and to changes in production systems, in particular through vocational training and retraining.

Article III-114

The Commission shall administer the Fund.

It shall be assisted in this task by a Committee presided over by a Member of the Commission and composed of representatives of Member States, trade unions and employers' organisations.

Article III-115

Implementing measures relating to the European Social Fund shall be enacted in European laws. Such laws shall be adopted after consultation of the Committee of the Regions and the Economic and Social Committee.

Section 3   ECONOMIC, SOCIAL AND TERRITORIAL COHESION

Article III-116

In order to promote its overall harmonious development, the Union shall develop and pursue its action leading to the strengthening of its economic, social and territorial cohesion.

In particular, the Union shall aim at reducing disparities between the levels of development of the various regions and the backwardness of the least favoured regions or islands, including rural areas.

Article III-117

Member States shall conduct their economic policies and shall coordinate them in such a way as, in addition, to attain the objectives set out in Article III-116. The formulation and implementation of the Union's policies and action and the implementation of the internal market shall take into account those objectives and shall contribute to their achievement. The Union shall also support the achievement of these objectives by the action it takes through the Structural Funds (European Agricultural Guidance and Guarantee Fund, Guidance Section; European Social Fund; European Regional Development Fund), the European Investment Bank and the other existing financial instruments.

The Commission shall submit a report to the European Parliament, the Council of Ministers, the Committee of the Regions and the Economic and Social Committee every three years on the progress made towards achieving economic, social and territorial cohesion and on the manner in which the various means provided for in this Article have contributed to it. This report shall, if necessary, be accompanied by appropriate proposals.

European laws or framework laws may establish any specific measure outside the Funds, without prejudice to measures adopted within the framework of the Union's other policies. They shall be adopted after consultation of the Committee of the Regions and the Economic and Social Committee.

Article III-118

The European Regional Development Fund is intended to help to redress the main regional imbalances in the Union through participation in the development and structural adjustment of regions whose development is lagging behind and in the conversion of declining industrial regions.

Article III-119

Without prejudice to Article III-120, European laws shall define the tasks, priority objectives and the organisation of the Structural Funds – which may involve grouping the Funds –, the general rules applicable to them and the provisions necessary to ensure their effectiveness and the coordination of the Funds with one another and with the other existing financial instruments.

A Cohesion Fund set up by a European law shall provide a financial contribution to projects in the fields of environment and trans-European networks in the area of transport infrastructure.

In all cases, such European laws shall be adopted after consultation of the Committee of the Regions and the Economic and Social Committee. The Council of Ministers shall act unanimously until 1 January 2007.

Article III-120

Implementing measures relating to the European Regional Development Fund shall be enacted in European laws. Such laws shall be adopted after consultation of the Committee of the Regions and the Economic and Social Committee.

With regard to the European Agricultural Guidance and Guarantee Fund, Guidance Section, and the European Social Fund, Articles III-127 and III-115 respectively shall apply.

Section 4   AGRICULTURE AND FISHERIES

Article III-121

The Union shall define and implement a common agriculture and fisheries policy.

"Agricultural products" means the products of the soil, of stockfarming and of fisheries and products of first-stage processing directly related to these products. References to the common agricultural policy or to agriculture, and the use of the term "agricultural", shall be understood as also referring to fisheries, having regard to the specific characteristics of this sector.

Article III-122

1.   The internal market shall extend to agriculture and trade in agricultural products.

2.   Save as otherwise provided in Articles III-123 to III-128, the rules laid down for the establishment of the internal market shall apply to agricultural products.

3.   The products listed in Annex I* shall be subject to Articles III-123 to III-128.

4.   The operation and development of the internal market for agricultural products must be accompanied by the establishment of a common agricultural policy.

Article III-123

1.   The objectives of the common agricultural policy shall be:

   (a) to increase agricultural productivity by promoting technical progress and by ensuring the rational development of agricultural production and the optimum utilisation of the factors of production, in particular labour;
   (b) thus to ensure a fair standard of living for the agricultural community, in particular by increasing the individual earnings of persons engaged in agriculture;
   (c) to stabilise markets;
   (d) to assure the availability of supplies;
   (e) to ensure that supplies reach consumers at reasonable prices.

---

* This Annex, which corresponds to Annex I to the TEC, is to be drawn up.

2.   In working out the common agricultural policy and the special methods for its application, account shall be taken of:

> (a) the particular nature of agricultural activity, which results from the social structure of agriculture and from structural and natural disparities between the various agricultural regions;
> (b) the need to effect the appropriate adjustments by degrees;
> (c) the fact that in the Member States agriculture constitutes a sector closely linked with the economy as a whole.

Article III-124

1.   In order to attain the objectives set out in Article III-123, a common organisation of agricultural markets shall be established.

This organisation shall take one of the following forms, depending on the product concerned:

> (a) common rules on competition;
> (b) compulsory coordination of the various national market organisations;
> (c) a European market organisation.

2.   The common organisation established in accordance with paragraph 1 may include all measures required to attain the objectives set out in Article III-123, in particular regulation of prices, aids for the production and marketing of the various products, storage and carryover arrangements and common machinery for stabilising imports or exports.

The common organisation shall be limited to pursuit of the objectives set out in Article III-123 and shall exclude any discrimination between producers or consumers within the Union.

Any common price policy shall be based on common criteria and uniform methods of calculation.

3.   In order to enable the common organisation referred to in paragraph 1 to attain its objectives, one or more agricultural guidance and guarantee funds may be set up.

Article III-125

To enable the objectives set out in Article III-123 to be attained, provision may be made within the framework of the common agricultural policy for measures such as:

> (a) an effective coordination of efforts in the spheres of vocational training, of research and of the dissemination of agricultural knowledge; this may include joint financing of projects or institutions;
>
> (b) joint measures to promote consumption of certain products.

Article III-126

1. The Section relating to rules on competition shall apply to production of and trade in agricultural products only to the extent determined by European laws or framework laws in accordance with Article III-127(2), having regard to the objectives set out in Article III-123.

2. The Council of Ministers, on a proposal from the Commission, may adopt a European regulation or decision authorising the granting of aid:

> (a) for the protection of enterprises handicapped by structural or natural conditions;
>
> (b) within the framework of economic development programmes.

Article III-127

1. The Commission shall submit proposals for working out and implementing the common agricultural policy, including the replacement of the national organisations by one of the forms of common organisation provided for in Article III-124(1), and for implementing the measures referred to in this Section.

These proposals shall take account of the interdependence of the agricultural matters mentioned in this Section.

2. European laws or framework laws shall establish the common organisation of the market provided for in Article III-124(1) and the other provisions necessary for the

achievement of the objectives of the common agricultural policy and the common fisheries policy. They shall be adopted after consultation of the Economic and Social Committee.

3.   The Council of Ministers, on a proposal from the Commission, shall adopt the European regulations or decisions on fixing prices, levies, aid and quantitative limitations and on the fixing and allocation of fishing opportunities.

4.   In accordance with paragraph 2, the national market organisations may be replaced by the common organisation provided for in Article III-124(1) if:

(a) the common organisation offers Member States which are opposed to this measure and which have an organisation of their own for the production in question equivalent safeguards for the employment and standard of living of the producers concerned, account being taken of the adjustments that will be possible and the specialisation that will be needed with the passage of time;

(b) such an organisation ensures conditions for trade within the Union similar to those existing in a national market.

5.   If a common organisation for certain raw materials is established before a common organisation exists for the corresponding processed products, such raw materials as are used for processed products intended for export to third countries may be imported from outside the Union.

Article III-128

Where in a Member State a product is subject to a national market organisation or to internal rules having equivalent effect which affect the competitive position of similar production in another Member State, a countervailing charge shall be applied by Member States to imports of this product coming from the Member State where such organisation or rules exist, unless that State applies a countervailing charge on export.

The Commission shall adopt European regulations or decisions fixing the amount of these charges at the level required to redress the balance; it may also authorise other measures, the conditions and details of which it shall determine.

Article III-129

1.   Union policy on the environment shall contribute to pursuit of the following objectives:

   (a) preserving, protecting and improving the quality of the environment;
   (b) protecting human health;
   (c) prudent and rational utilisation of natural resources;
   (d) promoting measures at international level to deal with regional or world-wide environmental problems.

2.   Union policy on the environment shall aim at a high level of protection taking into account the diversity of situations in the various regions of the Union. It shall be based on the precautionary principle and on the principles that preventive action should be taken, that environmental damage should as a priority be rectified at source and that the polluter should pay.

In this context, harmonisation measures answering environmental protection requirements shall include, where appropriate, a safeguard clause allowing Member States to take provisional steps, for non-economic environmental reasons, subject to a procedure of inspection by the Union.

3.   In preparing its policy on the environment, the Union shall take account of:

   (a) available scientific and technical data;
   (b) environmental conditions in the various regions of the Union;
   (c) the potential benefits and costs of action or lack of action;
   (d) the economic and social development of the Union as a whole and the balanced development of its regions.

4.   Within their respective spheres of competence, the Union and the Member States shall cooperate with third countries and with the competent international organisations. The arrangements for the Union's cooperation may be the subject of agreements between the Union and the third parties concerned, which shall be negotiated and concluded in accordance with Article III-272.

The previous subparagraph shall be without prejudice to Member States' competence to negotiate in international bodies and to conclude international agreements.

Article III-130

1.   European laws or framework laws shall establish what action is to be taken in order to achieve the objectives referred to in Article III-129. They shall be adopted after consultation of the Committee of the Regions and the Economic and Social Committee.

2.   By way of derogation from paragraph 1 and without prejudice to Article III-65, the Council of Ministers shall unanimously adopt European laws or framework laws establishing:

> (a) measures primarily of a fiscal nature;
> (b) measures affecting:
> (i)   town and country planning;
>
>> (ii) quantitative management of water resources or affecting, directly or indirectly, the availability of those resources;
>> (iii) land use, with the exception of waste management;
>
> (c) measures significantly affecting a Member State's choice between different energy sources and the general structure of its energy supply.

The Council of Ministers may unanimously adopt a European decision making the ordinary legislative procedure applicable to the matters referred to in the first subparagraph of this paragraph.

In all cases, the Council of Ministers shall act after consulting the European Parliament, the Committee of the Regions and the Economic and Social Committee.

3.   General action programmes which set out priority objectives to be attained shall be enacted by European laws. Such laws shall be adopted after consultation of the Committee of the Regions and the Economic and Social Committee.

The measures necessary for the implementation of these programmes shall be adopted under the terms of paragraph 1 or paragraph 2, according to the case.

4.   Without prejudice to certain measures adopted by the Union, the Member States shall finance and implement the environment policy.

5.   Without prejudice to the principle that the polluter should pay, if a measure based on paragraph 1 involves costs deemed disproportionate for the public authorities of a Member State, such measure shall provide in appropriate form for:

      a) temporary derogations, and/or
      b) financial support from the Cohesion Fund.

Article III-131

The protective provisions adopted pursuant to Article III-130 shall not prevent any Member State from maintaining or introducing more stringent protective provisions. Such provisions must be compatible with the Constitution. They shall be notified to the Commission.

Section 6   CONSUMER PROTECTION

Article III-132

1.   In order to promote the interests of consumers and to ensure a high level of consumer protection, the Union shall contribute to protecting the health, safety and economic interests of consumers, as well as to promoting their right to information, education and to organise themselves in order to safeguard their interests.

2.   The Union shall contribute to the attainment of the objectives referred to in paragraph 1 through:

      (a) measures adopted pursuant to Article III-65 in the context of the completion of the internal market;
      (b) measures which support, supplement and monitor the policy pursued by the Member States.

3. The measures referred to in paragraph 2(b) shall be enacted by European laws or framework laws. Such laws shall be adopted after consultation of the Economic and Social Committee.

4. Acts adopted pursuant to paragraph 3 shall not prevent any Member State from maintaining or introducing more stringent protective provisions. Such provisions must be compatible with the Constitution. They shall be notified to the Commission.

Section 7 **TRANSPORT**

Article III-133

The objectives of the Constitution shall, in matters governed by this Title, be pursued within the framework of a common transport policy.

Article III-134

European laws or framework laws shall implement Article III-133, taking into account the distinctive features of transport. They shall be adopted after consultation of the Committee of the Regions and the Economic and Social Committee.

Such European laws or framework laws shall contain:

    (a) common rules applicable to international transport to or from the territory of a Member State or passing across the territory of one or more Member States;
    (b) the conditions under which non-resident carriers may operate transport services within a Member State;
    (c) measures to improve transport safety;
    (d) any other appropriate measure.

Article III-135

Until the European laws or framework laws referred to in the first paragraph of Article III-134 have been adopted, no Member State may, unless the Council of Ministers has unanimously adopted a European decision granting a derogation, make the various provisions governing the subject on 1 January 1958 or, for acceding States, the date of their accession less favourable in their direct or indirect effect on carriers of other Member States as compared with carriers who are nationals of that State.

Article III-136

Aids shall be compatible with the Constitution if they meet the needs of coordination of transport or if they represent reimbursement for the discharge of certain obligations inherent in the concept of a public service.

Article III-137

Any measures adopted within the framework of the Constitution in respect of transport rates and conditions shall take account of the economic circumstances of carriers.

Article III-138

1. In the case of transport within the Union, discrimination which takes the form of carriers charging different rates and imposing different conditions for the carriage of the same goods over the same transport links on grounds of the Member State of origin or of destination of the goods in question shall be prohibited.

2. Paragraph 1 shall not prevent the adoption of other European laws or framework laws pursuant to the first paragraph of Article III-134.

3. The Council of Ministers, on a proposal from the Commission, shall adopt European regulations or decisions for implementing paragraph 1. It shall act after consulting the European Parliament and the Economic and Social Committee.

The Council of Ministers may in particular adopt the European regulations and decisions needed to enable the institutions to secure compliance with the rule laid down in paragraph 1 and to ensure that users benefit from it to the full.

4. The Commission, acting on its own initiative or on application by a Member State, shall investigate any cases of discrimination falling within paragraph 1 and, after consulting any Member State concerned, adopt the necessary European decisions within the framework of the European regulations and decisions referred to in paragraph 3.

Article III-139

1.　　　　The imposition by a Member State, in respect of transport operations carried out within the Union, of rates and conditions involving any element of support or protection in the interest of one or more particular undertakings or industries shall be prohibited, unless authorised by a European decision of the Commission.

2.　　　　The Commission, acting on its own initiative or on application by a Member State, shall examine the rates and conditions referred to in paragraph 1, taking account in particular of the requirements of an appropriate regional economic policy, the needs of underdeveloped areas and the problems of areas seriously affected by political circumstances on the one hand, and of the effects of such rates and conditions on competition between the different modes of transport on the other.

After consulting each Member State concerned, the Commission shall adopt the necessary European decisions.

3.　　　　The prohibition provided for in paragraph 1 shall not apply to tariffs fixed to meet competition.

Article III-140

Charges or dues in respect of the crossing of frontiers which are charged by a carrier in addition to the transport rates shall not exceed a reasonable level after taking the costs actually incurred thereby into account.

Member States shall endeavour to reduce these costs.

The Commission may make recommendations to Member States for the application of this Article.

Article III-141

The provisions of this Section shall not form an obstacle to the application of measures taken in the Federal Republic of Germany to the extent that such measures are required in order to compensate for the economic disadvantages caused by the division of Germany to the economy of certain areas of the Federal Republic affected by that division.

Article III-142

An Advisory Committee consisting of experts designated by the governments of Member States shall be attached to the Commission. The Commission, whenever it considers it desirable, shall consult the Committee on transport matters.

Article III-143

1.   This Section shall apply to transport by rail, road and inland waterway.

2.   European laws or framework laws may lay down appropriate measures for sea and air transport. They shall be adopted after consultation of the Committee of the Regions and the Economic and Social Committee.

Section 8   TRANS-EUROPEAN NETWORKS

Article III-144

1.   To help achieve the objectives referred to in Articles III-14 and III-116 and to enable citizens of the Union, economic operators and regional and local communities to derive full benefit from the setting-up of an area without internal frontiers, the Union shall contribute to the establishment and development of trans-European networks in the areas of transport, telecommunications and energy infrastructures.

2.   Within the framework of a system of open and competitive markets, action by the Union shall aim at promoting the interconnection and interoperability of nation-

al networks as well as access to such networks. It shall take account in particular of the need to link island, landlocked and peripheral regions with the central regions of the Union.

Article III-145

1.   In order to achieve the objectives referred to in Article III-144, the Union:

    (a) shall establish a series of guidelines covering the objectives, priorities and broad lines of measures envisaged in the sphere of trans-European networks; these guidelines shall identify projects of common interest;

    (b) shall implement any measures that may prove necessary to ensure the interoperability of the networks, in particular in the field of technical standardisation;

    (c) may support projects of common interest supported by Member States, which are identified in the framework of the guidelines referred to in point (a), particularly through feasibility studies, loan guarantees or interest-rate subsidies; the Union may also contribute, through the Cohesion Fund, to the financing of specific projects in Member States in the area of transport infrastructure.

The Union's activities shall take into account the potential economic viability of the projects.

2.   The guidelines and other measures referred to in paragraph 1 shall be enacted by European laws or framework laws. Such laws shall be adopted after consultation of the Committee of the Regions and the Economic and Social Committee.

Guidelines and projects of common interest which relate to the territory of a Member State shall require the agreement of the Member State concerned.

3.   Member States shall, in liaison with the Commission, coordinate among themselves the policies pursued at national level which may have a significant impact on the achievement of the objectives referred to in Article III-144. The Commission may, in close cooperation with the Member States, take any useful initiative to promote such coordination.

4.   The Union may cooperate with third countries to promote projects of mutual interest and to ensure the interoperability of networks.

Section 9   RESEARCH AND TECHNOLOGICAL DEVELOPMENT, AND SPACE

Article III-146

1.   The Union shall aim to strengthen the scientific and technological bases of Union industry and encourage it to become more competitive at international level, while promoting all the research activities deemed necessary by virtue of other Chapters of the Constitution.

2.   For this purpose, the Union shall, throughout the Union, encourage undertakings, including small and medium-sized undertakings, research centres and universities in their research and technological development activities of high quality; it shall support their efforts to cooperate with one another, aiming, notably, at enabling researchers to cooperate freely across borders and undertakings to exploit the internal market potential, in particular through the opening-up of national public contracts, the definition of common standards and the removal of legal and fiscal obstacles to that cooperation.

3.   All the Union's activities under the Constitution in the area of research and technological development, including demonstration projects, shall be decided on and implemented in accordance with this Section.

Article III-147

In pursuing these objectives, the Union shall carry out the following activities, complementing the activities carried out in the Member States:

(a) implementation of research, technological development and demonstration programmes, by promoting cooperation with and between undertakings, research centres and universities;

(b) promotion of cooperation in the field of the Union's research, technological development and demonstration with third countries and international organisations;

(c) dissemination and optimisation of the results of activities in the Union's research, technological development and demonstration;

(d) stimulation of the training and mobility of researchers in the Union.

Article III-148

1.   The Union and the Member States shall coordinate their research and technological development activities so as to ensure that national policies and the Union's policy are mutually consistent.

2.   In close cooperation with the Member States, the Commission may take any useful initiative to promote the coordination referred to in paragraph 1, in particular initiatives aiming at the establishment of guidelines and indicators, the organisation of exchange of best practice, and the preparation of the necessary elements for periodic monitoring and evaluation. The European Parliament shall be kept fully informed.

Article III-149

1.   A multiannual framework programme, setting out all the activities of the Union, shall be enacted by European laws. Such laws shall be adopted after consultation of the Economic and Social Committee.

The framework programme shall:

(a) establish the scientific and technological objectives to be achieved by the activities provided for in Article III-147 and fix the relevant priorities;

(b) indicate the broad lines of such activities;

(c) fix the maximum overall amount and the detailed rules for the Union's financial participation in the framework programme and the respective shares in each of the activities provided for.

2.   The framework programme shall be adapted or supplemented as the situation changes.

3.   The framework programme shall be implemented through specific programmes developed within each activity. Each specific programme shall define the

detailed rules for implementing it, fix its duration and provide for the means deemed necessary. The sum of the amounts deemed necessary, fixed in the specific programmes, may not exceed the overall maximum amount fixed for the framework programme and each activity.

4.　　　　　The Council of Ministers, on a proposal from the Commission, shall adopt the European regulations or decisions establishing the specific programmes. It shall act after consulting the European Parliament and the Economic and Social Committee.

Article III-150

For the implementation of the multiannual framework programme, European laws or framework laws shall establish:

    (a) the rules for the participation of undertakings, research centres and universities;
    (b) the rules governing the dissemination of research results.

Such European laws or framework laws shall be adopted after consultation of the Economic and Social Committee.

Article III-151

In implementing the multiannual framework programme, European laws may establish supplementary programmes involving the participation of certain Member States only, which shall finance them subject to possible participation by the Union.

Such laws shall determine the rules applicable to supplementary programmes, particularly as regards the dissemination of knowledge and access by other Member States. They shall be adopted after consultation of the Economic and Social Committee and with the agreement of the Member States concerned.

Article III-152

In implementing the multiannual framework programme, European laws may make provision, in agreement with the Member States concerned, for participation in research and development programmes undertaken by several Member States, including participation in the structures created for the execution of those programmes.

Such laws shall be adopted after consultation of the Economic and Social Committee.

Article III-153

In implementing the multiannual framework programme the Union may make provision for cooperation in the Union's research, technological development and demonstration with third countries or international organisations.

The detailed arrangements for such cooperation may be the subject of agreements between the Union and the third parties concerned, which shall be negotiated and concluded in accordance with Article III-227.

Article III-154

The Council of Ministers, on a proposal from the Commission, may adopt European regulations or decisions to set up joint undertakings or any other structure necessary for the efficient execution of the Union's research, technological development and demonstration programmes. It shall act after consulting the European Parliament and the Economic and Social Committee.

Article III-155

1.   To promote scientific and technical progress, industrial competitiveness and the implementation of its policies, the Union shall draw up a European space policy. To this end, it may promote joint initiatives, support research and technological development and coordinate the efforts needed for the exploration and exploitation of space.

2.   To contribute to attaining the objectives referred to in paragraph 1, European laws or framework laws shall establish the necessary measures, which may take the form of a European space programme.

Article III-156

At the beginning of each year the Commission shall send a report to the European Parliament and the Council of Ministers. The report shall include information on research and technological development activities and the dissemination of results during the previous year, and the work programme for the current year.

Section 10   ENERGY

Article III-157

1.   In establishing an internal market and with regard for the need to preserve and improve the environment, Union policy on energy shall aim to:

(a) ensure the functioning of the energy market,
(b) ensure security of energy supply in the Union, and
(c) promote energy efficiency and saving and the development of new and renewable forms of energy.

2.   The measures necessary to achieve the objectives in paragraph 1 shall be enacted in European laws or framework laws. Such laws shall be adopted after consultation of the Committee of the Regions and the Economic and Social Committee.

Such laws or framework laws shall not affect a Member State's choice between different energy sources and the general structure of its energy supply, without prejudice to Article III-130(2)(c).

Chapter IV   AREA OF FREEDOM, SECURITY AND JUSTICE

Section 1   GENERAL PROVISIONS

Article III-158

1.   The Union shall constitute an area of freedom, security and justice with respect for fundamental rights, taking into account the different legal traditions and systems of the Member States.

2.   It shall ensure the absence of internal border controls for persons and shall frame a common policy on asylum, immigration and external border control, based on solidarity between Member States, which is fair towards third-country nationals. For the purpose of this chapter, stateless persons shall be treated as third-country nationals.

3.   The Union shall endeavour to ensure a high level of security by measures to prevent and combat crime, racism and xenophobia, and measures for coordination and cooperation between police and judicial authorities and other competent authorities, as well as by the mutual recognition of judgments in criminal matters and, if necessary, the approximation of criminal laws.

4.   The Union shall facilitate access to justice, in particular by the principle of mutual recognition of judicial and extrajudicial decisions in civil matters.

Article III-159

The European Council shall define the strategic guidelines for legislative and operational planning within the area of freedom, security and justice.

Article III-160

1.   Member States' national Parliaments shall ensure that the proposals and legislative initiatives submitted under Sections 4 and 5 of this Chapter comply with the

principle of subsidiarity, in accordance with the arrangements in the Protocol on the application of the principles of subsidiarity and proportionality.

Member States' national Parliaments may participate in the evaluation mechanisms contained in Article III-161 and in the political monitoring of Europol and the evaluation of Eurojust's activities in accordance with Articles III-177 and III-174.

Article III-161

Without prejudice to Articles III-265 to III-267, the Council of Ministers may, on a proposal from the Commission, adopt European regulations or decisions laying down the arrangements whereby Member States, in collaboration with the Commission, conduct objective and impartial evaluation of the implementation of the Union policies referred to in this Chapter by Member States' authorities, in particular in order to facilitate full application of the principle of mutual recognition. The European Parliament and Member States' national Parliaments shall be informed of the content and results of the evaluation.

Article III-162

A standing committee shall be set up within the Council of Ministers in order to ensure that operational cooperation on internal security is promoted and strengthened within the Union. Without prejudice to Article III-247, it shall facilitate coordination of the action of Member States' competent authorities. Representatives of the Union bodies and agencies concerned may be involved in the proceedings of this committee. The European Parliament and Member States' national parliaments shall be kept informed of the proceedings.

Article III-163

This Chapter shall not affect the exercise of the responsibilities incumbent upon Member States with regard to maintaining law and order and safeguarding internal security.

Article III-164

The Council of Ministers shall adopt European regulations to ensure administrative coop-eration between the relevant departments of the Member States in the areas covered by this Chapter, as well as between those departments and the Commission. It shall act on a Commission proposal, without prejudice to Article III-165, and after consulting the European Parliament.

Article III-165

The acts referred to in Sections 4 and 5 of this Chapter shall be adopted:

> (a) on a proposal from the Commission, or
> (b) on the initiative of a quarter of the Member States.

Section 2   POLICIES ON BORDER CHECKS, ASYLUM AND IMMIGRATION

Article III-166

1.   The Union shall develop a policy with a view to:

> (a) ensuring the absence of any controls on persons, whatever their nation-ality, when crossing internal borders;
> (b) carrying out checks on persons and efficient monitoring of the crossing of external borders;
> (c) the gradual introduction of an integrated management system for exter-nal borders.

2.   For this purpose, European laws or framework laws shall establish measures concerning:

> (a) the common policy on visas and other short-stay residence permits;
> (b) the controls to which persons crossing external borders are subject;
> (c) the conditions under which nationals of third countries shall have the freedom to travel within the Union for a short period;

(d) any measure necessary for the gradual establishment of an integrated management system for external borders;

(e) the absence of any controls on persons, whatever their nationality, when crossing internal borders.

3.   This Article shall not affect the competence of the Member States concerning the geographical demarcation of their borders, in accordance with international law.

Article III-167

1.   The Union shall develop a common policy on asylum and temporary protection with a view to offering appropriate status to any third-country national requiring international protection and ensuring compliance with the principle of *non-refoulement*. This policy must be in accordance with the Geneva Convention of 28 July 1951 and the Protocol of 31 January 1967 relating to the status of refugees and other relevant treaties.

2.   For this purpose, European laws or framework laws shall lay down measures for a common European asylum system comprising:

(a) a uniform status of asylum for nationals of third countries, valid throughout the Union;

(b) a uniform status of subsidiary protection for nationals of third countries who, without obtaining European asylum, are in need of international protection;

(c) a common system of temporary protection for displaced persons in the event of a massive inflow;

(d) common procedures for the granting and withdrawing of uniform asylum or subsidiary protection status;

(e) criteria and mechanisms for determining which Member State is responsible for considering an application for asylum or subsidiary protection;

(f) standards concerning the conditions for the reception of applicants for asylum or subsidiary protection;

(g) partnership and cooperation with third countries for the purpose of managing inflows of people applying for asylum or subsidiary or temporary protection.

3.   In the event of one or more Member States being confronted by an emergency situation characterised by a sudden inflow of nationals of third countries, the Council of Ministers, on a proposal from the Commission, may adopt European regulations or decisions comprising provisional measures for the benefit of the Member State(s) concerned. It shall act after consulting the European Parliament.

Article III-168

1.   The Union shall develop a common immigration policy aimed at ensuring, at all stages, the efficient management of migration flows, fair treatment of third-country nationals residing legally in Member States, and the prevention of, and enhanced measures to combat, illegal immigration and trafficking in human beings.

2.   To this end, European laws or framework laws shall establish measures in the following areas:

> (a) the conditions of entry and residence, and standards on the issue by Member States of long-term visas and residence permits, including those for the purpose of family reunion;
> (b) the definition of the rights of third-country nationals residing legally in a Member State, including the conditions governing freedom of movement and of residence in other Member States;
> (c) illegal immigration and unauthorised residence, including removal and repatriation of persons residing without authorisation;
> (d) combating trafficking in persons, in particular women and children.

3.   The Union may conclude readmission agreements with third countries for the readmission of third-country nationals residing without authorisation to their countries of origin or provenance, in accordance with Article III-227.

4.   European laws or framework laws may establish measures to provide incentives and support for the action of Member States with a view to promoting the integration of third-country nationals residing legally in their territories, excluding any harmonisation of the laws and regulations of the Member States.

5.   This Article shall not affect the right of Member States to determine volumes of admission of third-country nationals coming from third countries to their territory in order to seek work, whether employed or self-employed.

Article III-169

The policies of the Union set out in this Section and their implementation shall be governed by the principle of solidarity and fair sharing of responsibility, including its financial implications, between the Member States. Whenever necessary, the acts of the Union adopted pursuant to this Section shall contain appropriate measures to give effect to this principle.

Section 3 JUDICIAL COOPERATION IN CIVIL MATTERS

Article III-170

1.   The Union shall develop judicial cooperation in civil matters having cross-border implications, based on the principle of mutual recognition of judgments and decisions in extrajudicial cases. Such cooperation may include the adoption of measures for the approximation of the laws and regulations of the Member States.

2.   To this end, laws or framework laws shall lay down measures aimed inter alia at ensuring:

> (a) the mutual recognition and enforcement between Member States of judgments and decisions in extrajudicial cases;
> (b) the cross-border service of judicial and extrajudicial documents;
> (c) the compatibility of the rules applicable in the Member States concerning conflict of laws and of jurisdiction;
> (d) cooperation in the taking of evidence;
> (e) a high level of access to justice;
> (f) the proper functioning of civil proceedings, if necessary by promoting the compatibility of the rules on civil procedure applicable in the Member States;
> (g) the development of alternative methods of dispute settlement;
> (h) support for the training of the judiciary and judicial staff.

3.   Notwithstanding paragraph 2, measures concerning family law with cross-border implications shall be laid down in a European law or framework law of the Council of Ministers. The Council of Ministers shall act unanimously after consulting the European Parliament.

The Council of Ministers, on a proposal from the Commission, may adopt a European decision determining those aspects of family law with cross-border implications which may be the subject of acts adopted by the ordinary legislative procedure. The Council of Ministers shall act unanimously after consulting the European Parliament.

Section 4 JUDICIAL COOPERATION IN CRIMINAL MATTERS

Article III-171

1.   Judicial cooperation in criminal matters in the Union shall be based on the principle of mutual recognition of judgments and judicial decisions and shall include the approximation of the laws and regulations of the Member States in the areas referred to in paragraph 2 and in Article III-172.

European laws or framework laws shall establish measures to:

(a) establish rules and procedures to ensure the recognition throughout the Union of all forms of judgments and judicial decisions;
(b) prevent and settle conflicts of jurisdiction between Member States;
(c) encourage the training of the judiciary and judicial staff;
(d) facilitate cooperation between judicial or equivalent authorities of the Member States in relation to proceedings in criminal matters and the enforcement of decisions.

2.   In order to facilitate mutual recognition of judgments and judicial decisions and police and judicial cooperation in criminal matters having a cross-border dimension, European framework laws may establish minimum rules concerning:

(a) mutual admissibility of evidence between Member States;
(b) the rights of individuals in criminal procedure;
(c) the rights of victims of crime;
(d) any other specific aspects of criminal procedure which the Council of Ministers has identified in advance by a European decision. The Council of Ministers shall act unanimously after obtaining the consent of the European Parliament.

Adoption of such minimum rules shall not prevent Member States from maintaining or introducing a higher level of protection for the rights of individuals in criminal procedure.

Article III-172

1.   European framework laws may establish minimum rules concerning the definition of criminal offences and sanctions in the areas of particularly serious crime with cross-border dimensions resulting from the nature or impact of such offences or from a special need to combat them on a common basis.

These areas of crime are the following: terrorism, trafficking in human beings and sexual exploitation of women and children, illicit drug trafficking, illicit arms trafficking, money laundering, corruption, counterfeiting of means of payment, computer crime and organised crime.

On the basis of developments in crime, the Council of Ministers may adopt a European decision identifying other areas of crime that meet the criteria specified in this paragraph. It shall act unanimously after obtaining the consent of the European Parliament.

2.   If the approximation of criminal legislation proves essential to ensure the effective implementation of a Union policy in an area which has been subject to harmonisation measures, European framework laws may establish minimum rules with regard to the definition of criminal offences and sanctions in the area concerned.

Without prejudice to Article III-165, such framework laws shall be adopted by the same procedure as was followed for the adoption of the harmonisation measures referred to in the preceding subparagraph.

Article III-173

European laws or framework laws may establish measures to promote and support the action of Member States in the field of crime prevention. Such measures shall not include the approximation of Member States' legislative and regulatory provisions.

Article III-174

1. Eurojust's mission shall be to support and strengthen coordination and cooperation between national prosecuting authorities in relation to serious crime affecting two or more Member States or requiring a prosecution on common bases, on the basis of operations conducted and information supplied by the Member States' authorities and by Europol.

2. European laws shall determine Eurojust's structure, workings, scope of action and tasks. Those tasks may include:

(a) the initiation and coordination of criminal prosecutions conducted by competent national authorities, particularly those relating to offences against the financial interests of the Union;

(b) the strengthening of judicial cooperation, including by resolution of conflicts of jurisdiction and by close cooperation with the European Judicial Network.

European laws shall also determine arrangements for involving the European Parliament and Member States' national Parliaments in the evaluation of Eurojust's activities.

3. In the prosecutions referred to in this Article, and without prejudice to Article III-175, formal acts of judicial procedure shall be carried out by the competent national officials.

Article III-175

1. In order to combat serious crime having a cross-border dimension, as well as crimes affecting the interests of the Union, a European law of the Council of Ministers may establish a European Public Prosecutor's Office from Eurojust. The Council of Ministers shall act unanimously after obtaining the consent of the European Parliament.

2. The European Public Prosecutor's Office shall be responsible for investigating, prosecuting and bringing to judgment, where appropriate in liaison with Europol, the perpetrators of and accomplices in serious crimes affecting more than one Member State and of offences against the Union's financial interests, as determined by the European law provided for in paragraph 1. It shall exercise the functions of prosecutor in the competent courts of the Member States in relation to such offences.

3.   The European law referred to in paragraph 1 shall determine the general rules applicable to the European Public Prosecutor's Office, the conditions governing the performance of its functions, the rules of procedure applicable to its activities, as well as those governing the admissibility of evidence, and the rules applicable to the judicial review of procedural measures taken by it in the performance of its functions.

Section 5 · POLICE COOPERATION

Article III-176

1.   The Union shall establish police cooperation involving all the Member States' competent authorities, including police, customs and other specialised law enforcement services in relation to the prevention, detection and investigation of criminal offences.

2.   To this end, European laws or framework laws may establish measures concerning:

(a) the collection, storage, processing, analysis and exchange of relevant information;

(b) support for the training of staff, and cooperation on the exchange of staff, on equipment and on research into crime-detection;

(c) common investigative techniques in relation to the detection of serious forms of organised crime.

3.   A European law or framework law of the Council of Ministers may establish measures concerning operational cooperation between the authorities referred to in this Article. The Council of Ministers shall act unanimously after consulting the European Parliament.

Article III-177

1.   Europol's mission is to support and strengthen action by the Member States' police authorities and other law enforcement services and their mutual cooperation in preventing and combating serious crime affecting two or more Member States, terrorism and forms of crime which affect a common interest covered by a Union policy.

2.   European laws shall determine Europol's structure, operation, field of action and tasks. These tasks may include:

> (a) the collection, storage, processing, analysis and exchange of information forwarded particularly by the authorities of the Member States or third countries or bodies;
>
> (b) the coordination, organisation and implementation of investigative and operational action carried out jointly with the Member States' competent authorities or in the context of joint investigative teams, where appropriate in liaison with Eurojust.

European laws shall also lay down the procedures for scrutiny of Europol's activities by the European Parliament, together with Member States' national parliaments.

3.   Any operational action by Europol must be carried out in liaison and in agreement with the authorities of the Member States whose territory is concerned. The application of coercive measures shall be the exclusive responsibility of the competent national authorities.

Article III-178

A European law or framework law of the Council of Ministers shall lay down the conditions and limitations under which the competent authorities of the Member States referred to in Articles III-171 and III-176 may operate in the territory of another Member State in liaison and in agreement with the authorities of that State. The Council of Ministers shall act unanimously after consulting the European Parliament.

Chapter V

AREAS WHERE THE UNION MAY TAKE COORDINATING, COMPLEMENTARY OR SUPPORTING ACTION

PUBLIC HEALTH

Article III-179

1.   A high level of human health protection shall be ensured in the definition and implementation of all the Union's policies and activities.

Action by the Union, which shall complement national policies, shall be directed towards improving public health, preventing human illness and diseases, and obviating sources of danger to physical and mental health. Such action shall cover the fight against the major health scourges, by promoting research into their causes, their transmission and their prevention, as well as health information and education.

The Union shall complement the Member States' action in reducing drugs-related health damage, including information and prevention.

2.   The Union shall encourage cooperation between the Member States in the areas referred to in this Article and, if necessary, lend support to their action.

Member States shall, in liaison with the Commission, coordinate among themselves their policies and programmes in the areas referred to in paragraph 1. The Commission may, in close contact with the Member States, take any useful initiative to promote such coordination, in particular initiatives aiming at the establishment of guidelines and indicators, the organisation of exchange of best practice, and the preparation of the necessary elements for periodic monitoring and evaluation. The European Parliament shall be kept fully informed.

3.   The Union and the Member States shall foster cooperation with third countries and the competent international organisations in the sphere of public health.

4.   European laws or framework laws shall contribute to the achievement of the objectives referred to in this Article by establishing the following measures in order to meet common safety concerns:

> (a) measures setting high standards of quality and safety of organs and sub-stances of human origin, blood and blood derivatives; these measures shall not prevent any Member State from maintaining or introducing more stringent protective measures;
>
> (b) measures in the veterinary and phytosanitary fields which have as their direct objective the protection of public health.

European laws or framework laws shall be adopted after consultation of the Committee of the Regions and the Economic and Social Committee.

5.   European laws or framework laws may also establish incentive measures designed to protect and improve human health and to combat the major cross-border health scourges, excluding any harmonisation of the laws and regulations of the Member States. It shall be adopted after consultation of the Committee of the Regions and the Economic and Social Committee.

6.   For the purposes set out in this Article, the Council of Ministers, on a pro-posal from the Commission, may also adopt recommendations.

7.   Union action in the field of public health shall fully respect the responsibil-ities of the Member States for the organisation and delivery of health services and med-ical care. In particular, measures referred to in paragraph 4(a) shall not affect national provisions on the donation or medical use of organs and blood.

Section 2   INDUSTRY

Article III-180

1.   The Union and the Member States shall ensure that the conditions neces-sary for the competitiveness of the Union's industry exist.

For that purpose, in accordance with a system of open and competitive markets, their action shall be aimed at:

    (a) speeding up the adjustment of industry to structural changes;

    (b) encouraging an environment favourable to initiative and to the development of undertakings throughout the Union, particularly small and medium-sized undertakings;

    (c) encouraging an environment favourable to cooperation between undertakings;

    (d) fostering better exploitation of the industrial potential of policies of innovation, research and technological development.

2.   The Member States shall consult each other in liaison with the Commission and, where necessary, shall coordinate their action. The Commission may take any useful initiative to promote such coordination, in particular initiatives aiming at the establishment of guidelines and indicators, the organisation of exchange of best practice, and the preparation of the necessary elements for periodic monitoring and evaluation. The European Parliament shall be kept fully informed.

3.   The Union shall contribute to the achievement of the objectives set out in paragraph 1 through the policies and activities it pursues under other provisions of the Constitution. European laws or framework laws may establish specific measures in support of action taken in the Member States to achieve the objectives set out in paragraph 1, excluding any harmonisation of the laws and regulations of the Member States. They shall be adopted after consultation of the Economic and Social Committee.

This Section shall not provide a basis for the introduction by the Union of any measure which could lead to distortion of competition or contains tax provisions or provisions relating to the rights and interests of employed persons.

Section 3   CULTURE

Article III-181

1.   The Union shall contribute to the flowering of the cultures of the Member States, while respecting their national and regional diversity and at the same time bringing the common cultural heritage to the fore.

2.	Action by the Union shall be aimed at encouraging cooperation between Member States and, if necessary, supporting and complementing their action in the following areas:

> (a) improvement of the knowledge and dissemination of the culture and history of the European peoples;
> (b) conservation and safeguarding of cultural heritage of European significance;
> (c) non-commercial cultural exchanges;
> (d) artistic and literary creation, including in the audiovisual sector.

3.	The Union and the Member States shall foster cooperation with third countries and the competent international organisations in the sphere of culture, in particular the Council of Europe.

4.	The Union shall take cultural aspects into account in its action under other provisions of the Constitution, in particular in order to respect and to promote the diversity of its cultures.

5.	In order to contribute to the achievement of the objectives referred to in this Article:

> (a) European laws or framework laws shall establish incentive actions, excluding any harmonisation of the laws and regulations of the Member States. They shall be adopted after consultation of the Committee of the Regions;
> (b) the Council of Ministers, on a proposal from the Commission, shall adopt recommendations.

Section 4 EDUCATION, VOCATIONAL TRAINING, YOUTH AND SPORT

Article III-182

1.	The Union shall contribute to the development of quality education by encouraging cooperation between Member States and, if necessary, by supporting and complementing their action. It shall fully respect the responsibility of the Member States for the content of teaching and the organisation of education systems and their cultural and linguistic diversity.

The Union shall contribute to the promotion of European sporting issues, given the social and educational function of sport.

2.   Union action shall be aimed at:

(a) developing the European dimension in education, particularly through the teaching and dissemination of the languages of the Member States;
(b) encouraging mobility of students and teachers, inter alia by encouraging the academic recognition of diplomas and periods of study;
(c) promoting cooperation between educational establishments;
(d) developing exchanges of information and experience on issues common to the education systems of the Member States;
(e) encouraging the development of youth exchanges and of exchanges of socio-educational instructors and encouraging the participation of young people in democratic life in Europe.
(f) encouraging the development of distance education;
(g) developing the European dimension in sport, by promoting fairness in competitions and cooperation between sporting bodies and by protecting the physical and moral integrity of sportsmen and sportswomen, especially young sportsmen and sportswomen.

3.   The Union and the Member States shall foster cooperation with third countries and the competent international organisations in the field of education, in particular the Council of Europe.

4.   In order to contribute to the achievement of the objectives referred to in this Article,

(a) European laws or framework laws shall establish incentive actions, excluding any harmonisation of the laws and regulations of the Member States. They shall be adopted after consultation of the Committee of the Regions and the Economic and Social Committee.
(b) the Council of Ministers, on a proposal from the Commission, shall adopt recommendations.

Article III-183

1.   The Union shall implement a vocational training policy which shall support and complement the action of the Member States, while fully respecting the responsibility of the Member States for the content and organisation of vocational training.

2.   Union action shall aim to:

(a) facilitate adaptation to industrial change, in particular through vocational training and retraining;

(b) improve initial and continuing vocational training in order to facilitate vocational integration and reintegration into the labour market;

(c) facilitate access to vocational training and encourage mobility of instructors and trainees and particularly young people;

(d) stimulate cooperation on training between educational or training establishments and firms;

(e) develop exchanges of information and experience on issues common to the training systems of the Member States.

3.   The Union and the Member States shall foster cooperation with third countries and the competent international organisations in the sphere of vocational training.

4.   European laws or framework laws shall contribute to the achievement of the objectives referred to in this Article, excluding any harmonisation of the laws and regulations of the Member States. They shall be adopted after consultation of the Committee of the Regions and the Economic and Social Committee.

Section 5   CIVIL PROTECTION

Article III-184

1.   The Union shall encourage cooperation between Member States in order to improve the effectiveness of systems for preventing and protecting against natural or man-made disasters within the Union.

Union action shall aim to:

(a) support and complement Member States' action at national, regional and local level in risk prevention, in preparing their civil-protection personnel and in responding to natural or man-made disasters;

(b) promote swift, effective operational cooperation between national civil-protection services;

(c) promote consistency in international civil-protection work.

2.　　　　The measures necessary to help achieve the objectives referred to in paragraph 1 shall be enacted in European laws or framework laws, excluding any harmonisation of the laws and regulations of the Member States.

Section 6　　ADMINISTRATIVE COOPERATION

Article III-185

1.　　　　Effective national implementation of Union law by the Member States, which is essential for the proper functioning of the Union, shall be regarded as a matter of common interest.

2.　　　　The Union may support the efforts of Member States to improve their administrative capacity to implement Union law. Such action may include facilitation of exchange of information and of civil servants as well as supporting training schemes. No Member State shall be obliged to avail itself of such support. European laws shall establish the necessary measures to this end, excluding any harmonisation of the laws and regulations of the Member States.

3.　　　　This Article shall be without prejudice to the obligations of the Member States to implement Union law or to the prerogatives and duties of the Commission. It shall also be without prejudice to other provisions of the Constitution providing for administrative cooperation among the Member States and between them and the Union.

ASSOCIATION OF THE OVERSEAS
COUNTRIES AND TERRITORIES

Article III-186

The non-European countries and territories which have special relations with Denmark,
France, the Netherlands and the United Kingdom shall be associated with the Union.
These countries and territories (hereinafter called the "countries and territories") are
listed in Annex II*.

The purpose of association shall be to promote the economic and social development of
the countries and territories and to establish close economic relations between them and
the Union as a whole.

Association shall serve primarily to further the interests and prosperity of the inhabitants
of these countries and territories in order to lead them to the economic, social and cultural development to which they aspire.

Article III-187

Association shall have the following objectives:

(a) Member States shall apply to their trade with the countries and territories the same treatment as they accord each other pursuant to the
Constitution;

(b) Each country or territory shall apply to its trade with Member States
and with the other countries and territories the same treatment as that
which it applies to the European State with which it has special relations;

(c) Member States shall contribute to the investments required for the progressive development of these countries and territories;

(d) For investments financed by the Union, participation in tenders and
supplies shall be open on equal terms to all natural and legal persons
who are nationals of a Member State or of one of the countries and territories;

---

* This Annex, which corresponds to Annex II to the TEC, is to be drawn up.

(e) In relations between Member States and the countries and territories, the right of establishment of nationals and companies or firms shall be regulated in accordance with the provisions and procedures laid down in the Subsection relating to the right of establishment and on a non-discriminatory basis, subject to any special measures adopted pursuant to Article III-191.

Article III-188

1. Customs duties on imports into the Member States of goods originating in the countries and territories shall be prohibited in conformity with the prohibition of customs duties between Member States provided for by the Constitution.

2. Customs duties on imports into each country or territory from Member States or from the other countries or territories shall be prohibited in accordance with Article III-38.

3. The countries and territories may, however, levy customs duties which meet the needs of their development and industrialisation or produce revenue for their budgets.

The duties referred to in the first subparagraph may not exceed the level of those imposed on imports of products from the Member State with which each country or territory has special relations.

4. Paragraph 2 shall not apply to countries and territories which, by reason of the particular international obligations by which they are bound, already apply a non-discriminatory customs tariff.

5. The introduction of or any change in customs duties imposed on goods imported into the countries and territories shall not, either in law or in fact, give rise to any direct or indirect discrimination between imports from the various Member States.

Article III-189

If the level of the duties applicable to goods from a third country on entry into a country or territory is liable, when Article III-188(1) has been applied, to cause deflections of trade to the detriment of any Member State, the latter may request the Commission to propose to the other Member States that they take the necessary steps to remedy the situation.

Article III-190

Subject to the provisions relating to public health, public security or public policy, freedom of movement within Member States for workers from the countries and territories, and within the countries and territories for workers from Member States, shall be regulated by measures adopted in accordance with Article III-191.

Article III-191

The Council of Ministers shall adopt unanimously, on the basis of the experience acquired under the association of the countries and territories with the Union, European regulations and decisions as regards the detailed rules and the procedure for the association of the countries and territories with the Union.

Article III-192

Articles III-186 to III-191 shall apply to Greenland, subject to the specific provisions set out in the Protocol on special arrangements for Greenland.

THE UNION'S EXTERNAL ACTION

Chapter I

PROVISIONS HAVING GENERAL APPLICATION

Article III-193

1.   The Union's action on the international scene shall be guided by, and designed to advance in the wider world, the principles which have inspired its own creation, development and enlargement: democracy, the rule of law, the universality and indivisibility of human rights and fundamental freedoms, respect for human dignity, equality and solidarity, and for international law in accordance with the principles of the United Nations Charter.

The Union shall seek to develop relations and build partnerships with third countries, and international, regional or global organisations, which share these values. It shall promote multilateral solutions to common problems, in particular in the framework of the United Nations.

2.   The Union shall define and pursue common policies and actions, and shall work for a high degree of cooperation in all fields of international relations, in order to:

(a) safeguard the common values, fundamental interests, security, independence and integrity of the Union;

(b) consolidate and support democracy, the rule of law, human rights and international law;

(c) preserve peace, prevent conflicts and strengthen international security, in conformity with the principles of the United Nations Charter;

(d) foster the sustainable economic, social and environmental development of developing countries, with the primary aim of eradicating poverty;

(e) encourage the integration of all countries into the world economy, including through the progressive abolition of restrictions on international trade;

(f) help develop international measures to preserve and improve the quality of the environment and the sustainable management of global natural resources, in order to ensure sustainable development;

(g) assist populations, countries and regions confronting natural or man-made disasters;

(h) promote an international system based on stronger multilateral cooperation and good global governance.

3.   The Union shall respect the principles and pursue the objectives listed in paragraphs 1 and 2 in the development and implementation of the different areas of the Union's external action covered by this Title and the external aspects of its other policies.

The Union shall ensure consistency between the different areas of its external action and between these and its other policies. The Council of Ministers and the Commission, assisted by the Union Minister for Foreign Affairs, shall ensure that consistency and shall cooperate to that effect.

Article III-194

1.   On the basis of the principles and objectives referred to in Article III-193, the European Council shall identify the strategic interests and objectives of the Union.

European decisions of the European Council on the strategic interests and objectives of the Union shall relate to the common foreign and security policy and to other areas of the external action of the Union. Such decisions may concern the relations of the Union with a specific country or region or may be thematic in approach. They shall define their duration, and the means to be made available by the Union and the Member States.

The European Council shall act unanimously on a recommendation from the Council of Ministers, adopted by the latter under the arrangements laid down for each area. European decisions of the European Council shall be implemented in accordance with the procedures provided for by the Constitution.

2.   The Union Minister for Foreign Affairs, for the field of common foreign and security policy, and the Commission, for other fields of external action, may submit joint proposals to the Council of Ministers.

Chapter II

COMMON FOREIGN
AND SECURITY POLICY

Article III-195

1.   In the context of the principles and objectives of its external action, the Union shall define and implement a common foreign and security policy covering all areas of foreign and security policy.

2.   The Member States shall support the common foreign and security policy actively and unreservedly in a spirit of loyalty and mutual solidarity.

The Member States shall work together to enhance and develop their mutual political solidarity. They shall refrain from any action which is contrary to the interests of the Union or likely to impair its effectiveness as a cohesive force in international relations.

The Council of Ministers and the Union Minister for Foreign Affairs shall ensure that these principles are complied with.

3.   The Union shall conduct the common foreign and security policy by:

(a) defining the general guidelines;
(b) adopting European decisions on:

  (i) actions of the Union,
  (ii) positions of the Union,
  (iii) implementation of actions and positions;

(c) strengthening systematic cooperation between Member States in the conduct of policy.

Article III-196

1.   The European Council shall define the general guidelines for the common foreign and security policy, including for matters with defence implications.

If international developments so require, the President of the European Council shall convene an extraordinary meeting of the European Council in order to define the strategic lines of the Union's policy in the face of such developments.

2.   The Council of Ministers shall adopt the European decisions necessary for defining and implementing the common foreign and security policy on the basis of the general guidelines and strategic lines defined by the European Council.

Article III-197

1.   The Union Minister for Foreign Affairs, who shall chair the Council of Ministers for Foreign Affairs, shall contribute through his or her proposals towards the preparation of the common foreign and security policy and shall ensure implementation of the European decisions adopted by the European Council and the Council of Ministers.

2.   For matters relating to the common foreign and security policy, the Union shall be represented by the Union Minister for Foreign Affairs. He or she shall conduct political dialogue on the Union's behalf and shall express the Union's position in international organisations and at international conferences.

3.   In fulfilling his or her mandate, the Union Minister for Foreign Affairs shall be assisted by a European External Action Service. This service shall work in cooperation with the diplomatic services of the Member States[1].

Article III-198

1.   Where the international situation requires operational action by the Union, the Council of Ministers shall adopt the necessary European decisions. Such decisions shall lay down the objectives, the scope, the means to be made available to the Union, if necessary the duration, and the conditions for implementation of the action.

If there is a change in circumstances having a substantial effect on a question subject to such a European decision, the Council of Ministers shall review the principles and objectives of the action and adopt the necessary European decisions. As long as the Council of Ministers has not acted, the European decision on action by the Union shall stand.

---

[1] See the Declaration on the creation of a European External Action Service.

2.   Such European decisions shall commit the Member States in the positions they adopt and in the conduct of their activity.

3.   Whenever there is any plan to adopt a national position or take national action pursuant to a European decision as referred to in paragraph 1, information shall be provided in time to allow, if necessary, for prior consultations within the Council of Ministers. The obligation to provide prior information shall not apply to arrangements which are merely a national transposition of European decisions.

4.   In cases of imperative need arising from changes in the situation and failing a new European decision, Member States may make the necessary arrangements as a matter of urgency, having regard to the general objectives of the European decision referred to in paragraph 1. The Member State concerned shall inform the Council of Ministers immediately of any such arrangements.

5.   Should there be any major difficulties in implementing a European decision as referred to in this Article, a Member State shall refer them to the Council of Ministers which shall discuss them and seek appropriate solutions. Such solutions shall not run counter to the objectives of the action or impair its effectiveness.

Article III-199

The Council of Ministers shall adopt European decisions which shall define the approach of the Union to a particular matter of a geographical or thematic nature. Member States shall ensure that their national policies conform to the positions of the Union.

Article III-200

1.   Any Member State, the Union Minister for Foreign Affairs, or that Minister with the Commission's support, may refer to the Council of Ministers any question relating to the common foreign and security policy and may submit proposals to it.

2.   In cases requiring a rapid decision, the Union Minister for Foreign Affairs, of the Minister's own motion or at the request of a Member State, shall convene an extraordinary meeting of the Council of Ministers within forty-eight hours or, in an emergency, within a shorter period.

1.　　　　European decisions referred to in this Chapter shall be adopted by the Council of Ministers acting unanimously. Abstentions by members present in person or represented shall not prevent the adoption of such decisions.

When abstaining in a vote, any member of the Council of Ministers may qualify its abstention by making a formal declaration. In that case, it shall not be obliged to apply the European decision, but shall accept that the latter commits the Union. In a spirit of mutual solidarity, the Member State concerned shall refrain from any action likely to conflict with or impede Union action based on that decision and the other Member States shall respect its position. If the members of the Council of Ministers qualifying their abstention in this way represent at least one third of the Member States representing at least one third of the population of the Union, the decision shall not be adopted.

2.　　　　By derogation from paragraph 1, the Council of Ministers shall act by qualified majority:

(a) when adopting European decisions on Union actions and positions on the basis of a European decision of the European Council relating to the Union's strategic interests and objectives, as referred to in Article III-194(1);

(b) when adopting a decision on a Union action or position, on a proposal which the Minister has put to it following a specific request to him or her from the European Council made on its own initiative or that of the Minister;

(c) when adopting any European decision implementing a Union action or position;

(d) when adopting a European decision concerning the appointment of a special representative in accordance with Article III-203.

If a member of the Council of Ministers declares that, for vital and stated reasons of national policy, it intends to oppose the adoption of a European decision to be adopted by qualified majority, a vote shall not be taken. The Union Minister for Foreign Affairs will, in close consultation with the Member State involved, search for a solution acceptable to it. If he or she does not succeed, the Council of Ministers may, acting by a qualified majority, request that the matter be referred to the European Council for decision by unanimity.

3.   The European Council may decide unanimously that the Council of Ministers shall act by a qualified majority in cases other than those referred to in paragraph 2.

4.   Paragraphs 2 and 3 shall not apply to decisions having military or defence implications.

Article III-202

1.   When the Union has defined a common approach within the meaning of Article I-39(5), the Union Minister for Foreign Affairs and the Ministers for Foreign Affairs of the Member States shall coordinate their activities within the Council of Ministers.

2.   The diplomatic missions of the Member States and the delegations of the Union shall cooperate in third countries and in international organisations and shall contribute to formulating and implementing a common approach.

Article III-203

The Council of Ministers shall, whenever it deems it necessary, appoint, on the initiative of the Union Minister for Foreign Affairs, a special representative with a mandate in relation to particular policy issues. The special representative shall carry out his or her mandate under the authority of the Union Minister for Foreign Affairs.

Article III-204

The Union may conclude agreements with one or more States or international organisations pursuant to this Chapter, in accordance with the procedure described in Article III-227.

Article III-205

1.   The Union Minister for Foreign Affairs shall consult the European Parliament on the main aspects and the basic choices of the common foreign and security policy, including the common security and defence policy, and shall ensure that the views of the European Parliament are duly taken into consideration. The European Parliament shall be kept regularly informed by the Union Minister for Foreign Affairs of the development of the common foreign and security policy, including the common security and defence policy. Special representatives may be involved in briefing the European Parliament.

2.   The European Parliament may ask questions of the Council of Ministers and of the Union Minister for Foreign Affairs or make recommendations to them. Twice a year it shall hold a debate on progress in implementing the common foreign and security policy, including the common security and defence policy.

Article III-206

1.   Member States shall coordinate their action in international organisations and at international conferences. They shall uphold the Union's positions in such fora. The Union Minister for Foreign Affairs shall organise this coordination.

In international organisations and at international conferences where not all the Member States participate, those which do take part shall uphold the Union's positions.

2.   Without prejudice to paragraph 1 and Article III-198(3), Member States represented in international organisations or international conferences where not all the Member States participate shall keep the latter, as well as the Union Minister for Foreign Affairs, informed of any matter of common interest.

Member States which are also members of the United Nations Security Council shall concert and keep the other Member States and the Union Minister for Foreign Affairs fully informed. Member States which are members of the Security Council will, in the execution of their functions, defend the positions and the interests of the Union, without prejudice to their responsibilities under the provisions of the United Nations Charter.

When the Union has defined a position on a subject which is on the United Nations Security Council agenda, those Member States which sit on the Security Council shall request that the Union Minister for Foreign Affairs be asked to present the Union's position.

Article III-207

The diplomatic and consular missions of the Member States and the Union delegations in third countries and international conferences, and their representations to international organisations, shall cooperate in ensuring that the European decisions relating to Union positions and actions adopted by the Council of Ministers are complied with and implemented. They shall step up cooperation by exchanging information and carrying out joint assessments.

They shall contribute to the implementation of the provisions referred to in Article I-8(2) on the rights of European citizens to protection in the territory of a third country and the measures adopted pursuant to Article III-11.

Article III-208

Without prejudice to Article III-247, a Political and Security Committee shall monitor the international situation in the areas covered by the common foreign and security policy and contribute to the definition of policies by delivering opinions to the Council of Ministers at the request of the latter, or of the Union Minister for Foreign Affairs, or on its own initiative. It shall also monitor the implementation of agreed policies, without prejudice to the responsibility of the Union Minister for Foreign Affairs.

Within the scope of this Chapter, this Committee shall exercise, under the responsibility of the Council of Ministers and of the Union Minister for Foreign Affairs, political control and strategic direction of crisis management operations, as defined in Article III-210.

The Council of Ministers may authorise the Committee, for the purpose and for the duration of a crisis management operation, as determined by the Council of Ministers, to take the relevant measures concerning the political control and strategic direction of the operation.

Article III-209

The implementation of the common foreign and security policy shall not affect the competences listed in Articles I-12 to I-14 and I-16. Likewise, the implementation of the policies listed in those articles shall not affect the competence referred to in Article I-15.

The Court of Justice shall have jurisdiction to monitor compliance with this Article.

Article III-210

1.   The tasks referred to in Article I-40(1), in the course of which the Union may use civilian and military means, shall include joint disarmament operations, humanitarian and rescue tasks, military advice and assistance tasks, conflict prevention and peace-keeping tasks, tasks of combat forces in crisis management, including peacemaking and post-conflict stabilisation. All these tasks may contribute to the fight against terrorism, including by supporting third countries in combating terrorism in their territories.

2.   The Council of Ministers, acting unanimously, shall adopt European decisions relating to the tasks referred to in paragraph 1, defining their objectives and scope and the general conditions for their implementation. The Union Minister for Foreign Affairs, acting under the authority of the Council of Ministers and in close and constant contact with the Political and Security Committee, shall ensure coordination of the civilian and military aspects of such tasks.

Article III-211

1.   Within the framework of the European decisions adopted in accordance with Article III-210, the Council of Ministers may entrust the implementation of a task to a group of Member States having the necessary capability and the desire to undertake the task. Those Member States in association with the Union Minister for Foreign Affairs shall agree between themselves on the management of the task.

2.   The Council of Ministers shall be regularly informed by the Member States participating in the task of its progress. Should the completion of the task involve major new consequences or require amendment of the objective, scope and conditions for implementation adopted by the Council of Ministers under Article III-210, the Member States participating shall refer the matter to the Council of Ministers forthwith. In such cases, the Council of Ministers shall adopt the necessary European decisions.

Article III-212

1.   The European Armaments, Research and Military Capabilities Agency, subject to the authority of the Council of Ministers, shall have as its task to:

> (a) contribute to identifying the Member States' military capability objectives and evaluating observance of the capability commitments given by the Member States;
>
> (b) promote harmonisation of operational needs and adoption of effective, compatible procurement methods;
>
> (c) propose multilateral projects to fulfil the objectives in terms of military capabilities, ensure coordination of the programmes implemented by the Member States and management of specific cooperation programmes;
>
> (d) support defence technology research, and coordinate and plan joint research activities and the study of technical solutions meeting future operational needs;
>
> (e) contribute to identifying and, if necessary, implementing any useful measure for strengthening the industrial and technological base of the defence sector and for improving the effectiveness of military expenditure.

2.   The Agency shall be open to all Member States wishing to be part of it. The Council of Ministers, acting by qualified majority, shall adopt a European decision defining the Agency's statute, seat and operational rules. That decision should take account of the level of effective participation in the Agency's activities. Specific groups shall be set up within the Agency bringing together Member States engaged in joint projects. The Agency shall carry out its tasks in liaison with the Commission where necessary.

Article III-213

1.   The Member States listed in the Protocol [*title*], which fulfil higher military capability criteria and wish to enter into more binding commitments in this matter with a view to the most demanding tasks, hereby establish structured cooperation between themselves within the meaning of Article I-40(6). The military capability criteria and commitments which those Member States have defined are set out in that Protocol.

2.   If a Member State wishes to participate in such cooperation at a later stage, and thus subscribe to the obligations it imposes, it shall inform the European Council of its intention. The Council of Ministers shall deliberate at the request of that Member State. Only the members of the Council of Ministers that represent the Member States taking part in structured cooperation shall participate in the vote.

3.   When the Council of Ministers adopts European decisions relating to matters covered by structured cooperation, only the members of the Council of Ministers that represent the Member States taking part in structured cooperation shall participate in the deliberations and the adoption of such decisions. The Union Minister for Foreign Affairs shall attend the deliberations. The representatives of the other Member States shall be duly and regularly informed by the Union Minister for Foreign Affairs of developments in structured cooperation.

4.   The Council of Ministers may ask the Member States participating in such cooperation to carry out at Union level a task referred to in Article III-210.

5.   Notwithstanding the previous paragraphs, the appropriate provisions relating to enhanced cooperation shall apply to the structured cooperation governed by this Article.

Article III-214

1.   The closer cooperation on mutual defence provided for in Article I-40(7) shall be open to all Member States of the Union. A list of Member States participating in closer cooperation shall be set out in the declaration [*title*]. If a Member State wishes to take part in such cooperation at a later stage, and thus accept the obligations it imposes, it shall inform the European Council of its intention and shall subscribe to that declaration.

2.   A Member State participating in such cooperation which is the victim of armed aggression on its territory shall inform the other participating States of the situation and may request aid and assistance from them. Participating Member States shall meet at ministerial level, assisted by their representatives on the Political and Security Committee and the Military Committee.

3.   The United Nations Security Council shall be informed immediately of any armed aggression and the measures taken as a result.

4.   This Article shall not affect the rights and obligations resulting, for the Member States concerned, from the North Atlantic Treaty.

Section 2   FINANCIAL PROVISIONS

Article III-215

1.   Administrative expenditure which the provisions referred to in this Chapter entail for the institutions shall be charged to the Union budget.

2.   Operating expenditure to which the implementation of those provisions gives rise shall also be charged to the Union budget, except for such expenditure arising from operations having military or defence implications and cases where the Council of Ministers decides otherwise.

In cases where expenditure is not charged to the Union's budget it shall be charged to the Member States in accordance with the gross national product scale, unless the Council of Ministers decides otherwise. As for expenditure arising from operations having military or defence implications, Member States whose representatives in the Council of Ministers have made a formal declaration under Article III-201(1), second subparagraph, shall not be obliged to contribute to the financing thereof.

3.   The Council of Ministers shall adopt a European decision establishing the specific procedures for guaranteeing rapid access to appropriations in the Union budget for urgent financing of initiatives in the framework of the common foreign and security policy, and in particular for preparatory activities for tasks as referred to in Article I-40(1). It shall act after consulting the European Parliament.

Preparatory activities for tasks as referred to in Article I-40(1) which are not charged to the Union budget shall be financed by a start-up fund made up of Member States' contributions.

The Council of Ministers shall adopt by a qualified majority on a proposal from the Union Minister for Foreign Affairs European decisions establishing:

(a) the procedures for setting up and financing the start-up fund, in particular the amounts allocated to the fund and the procedures for reimbursement;

  (b) the procedures for administering the start-up fund;

  (c) the financial control procedures.

When it is planning a task as referred to in Article I-40(1) which cannot be charged to the Union's budget, the Council of Ministers shall authorise the Union Minister for Foreign Affairs to use the fund. The Union Minister for Foreign Affairs shall report to the Council of Ministers on the implementation of this remit.

Chapter III COMMON COMMERCIAL POLICY

Article III-216

By establishing a customs union between the Member States, the Union aims to contribute, in the common interest, to the harmonious development of world trade, the progressive abolition of restrictions on international trade and on foreign direct investment, and the lowering of customs and other barriers.

Article III-217

1.   The common commercial policy shall be based on uniform principles, particularly with regard to changes in tariff rates, the conclusion of tariff and trade agreements relating to trade in goods and services and the commercial aspects of intellectual property, foreign direct investment, the achievement of uniformity in measures of liberalisation, export policy and measures to protect trade such as those to be taken in the event of dumping or subsidies. The common commercial policy shall be conducted in the context of the principles and objectives of the Union's external action.

2.   European laws or framework laws shall establish the measures required to implement the common commercial policy.

3.   Where agreements with one or more States or international organisations need to be negotiated and concluded, the relevant provisions of Article III-227 shall apply. The Commission shall make recommendations to the Council of Ministers, which shall authorise the Commission to open the necessary negotiations. The Council of Ministers and the Commission shall be responsible for ensuring that the agreements negotiated are compatible with internal Union policies and rules.

The Commission shall conduct these negotiations in consultation with a special committee appointed by the Council of Ministers to assist the Commission in this task and within the framework of such directives as the Council of Ministers may issue to it. The Commission shall report regularly to the special committee and to the European Parliament on the progress of negotiations.

4.　　　　For the negotiation and conclusion of agreements in the fields of trade in services involving the movement of persons and the commercial aspects of intellectual property, the Council of Ministers shall act unanimously where such agreements include provisions for which unanimity is required for the adoption of internal rules.

The Council shall also act unanimously for the negotiation and conclusion of agreements in the field of trade in cultural and audiovisual services, where these risk prejudicing the Union's cultural and linguistic diversity.

The negotiation and conclusion of international agreements in the field of transport shall be subject to the provisions of Section 7 of Chapter III of Title III and Article III-227.

5.　　　　The exercise of the competences conferred by this Article in the field of commercial policy shall not affect the delimitation of internal competences between the Union and the Member States, and shall not lead to harmonisation of legislative or regulatory provisions of Member States insofar as the Constitution excludes such harmonisation.

Chapter IV

COOPERATION WITH THIRD COUNTRIES AND HUMANITARIAN AID

DEVELOPMENT COOPERATION

Article III-218

1.   Union policy in the sphere of development cooperation shall be conducted within the framework of the principles and objectives of the Union's external action. The Union's development cooperation policy and that of the Member States complement and reinforce each other.

Union development cooperation policy shall have as its primary objective the reduction and, in the long term, the eradication of poverty. The Union shall take account of the objectives of development cooperation in the policies that it implements which are likely to affect developing countries.

2.   The Union and the Member States shall comply with the commitments and take account of the objectives they have approved in the context of the United Nations and other competent international organisations.

Article III-219

1.   European laws or framework laws shall establish the measures necessary for the implementation of development cooperation policy, which may relate to multiannual cooperation programmes with developing countries or programmes with a thematic approach.

2.   The Union may conclude with third countries and competent international organisations any agreement helping to achieve the objectives referred to in Article III-193. Such agreements shall be negotiated and concluded in accordance with Article III-227.

The first subparagraph shall be without prejudice to Member States' competence to negotiate in international bodies and to conclude international agreements.

3.   The European Investment Bank shall contribute, under the terms laid down in its Statute, to the implementation of the measures referred to in paragraph 1.

Article III-220

1.   In order to promote the complementarity and efficiency of their action, the Union and the Member States shall coordinate their policies on development cooperation and shall consult each other on their aid programmes, including in international organisations and during international conferences. They may undertake joint action. Member States shall contribute if necessary to the implementation of Union aid programmes.

2.   The Commission may take any useful initiative to promote the coordination referred to in paragraph 1.

3.   Within their respective spheres of competence, the Union and the Member States shall cooperate with third countries and the competent international organisations.

Section 2   ECONOMIC, FINANCIAL AND TECHNICAL COOPERATION WITH THIRD COUNTRIES

Article III-221

1.   Without prejudice to the other provisions of the Constitution, and in particular those of Articles III-218 to III-220, the Union shall carry out economic, financial and technical cooperation measures, including financial aid in particular, with third countries other than developing countries. Such measures shall be consistent with the development policy of the Union and shall be carried out within the framework of the principles and objectives of its external action. The Union's measures and those of the Member States shall complement and reinforce each other.

2.   European laws or framework laws shall establish the measures necessary for the implementation of paragraph 1.

3.   Within their respective spheres of competence, the Union and the Member States shall cooperate with third countries and the competent international organisations. The arrangements for Union cooperation may be the subject of agreements between the Union and the third parties concerned, which shall be negotiated and concluded pursuant to Article III-227. The Council of Ministers shall act unanimously for the association agreements referred to in Article III-226(2) and for the agreements with the States which are candidates for accession to the Union.

The first subparagraph shall be without prejudice to Member States' competence to negotiate in international bodies and to conclude international agreements.

Article III-222

When the situation in a third country requires urgent financial aid from the Union, the Council of Ministers shall adopt the necessary European decisions on a proposal from the Commission.

Section 3   HUMANITARIAN AID

Article III-223

1.   The Union's operations in the field of humanitarian aid shall be conducted within the framework of the principles and objectives of the external action of the Union. Such operations shall be intended to provide ad hoc assistance, relief and protection for people in third countries and victims of natural or man-made disasters, in order to meet the humanitarian needs resulting from these different situations. The Union's operations and those of the Member States shall complement and reinforce each other.

2.   Humanitarian aid operations shall be conducted in compliance with the principles of international humanitarian law, in particular the principles of impartiality and non-discrimination.

3.   European laws or framework laws shall establish the measures defining the framework within which the Union's humanitarian aid operations shall be implemented.

4. The Union may conclude with third countries and competent international organisations any agreement helping to achieve the objectives referred to in Article III-193. Such agreements shall be negotiated and concluded pursuant to Article III-227.

The first subparagraph shall be without prejudice to Member States' competence to negotiate in international bodies and to conclude international agreements.

5. In order to establish a framework for joint contributions from young Europeans to the humanitarian actions of the Union, a European Voluntary Humanitarian Aid Corps shall be set up. European law shall determine the rules and operation of the Corps.

6. The Commission may take any useful initiative to promote coordination between actions of the Union and those of the Member States, in order to enhance the efficiency and complementarity of Union and national humanitarian aid measures.

7. The Union shall ensure that its humanitarian operations are coordinated and consistent with those of international organisations and bodies, in particular those forming part of the United Nations system.

Chapter V   RESTRICTIVE MEASURES

Article III-224

1.   Where a European decision on a Union position or action adopted in accordance with the provisions on the common foreign and security policy in Chapter II of this Title provides for the interruption or reduction, in part or completely, of economic and financial relations with one or more third countries, the Council of Ministers, acting by a qualified majority on a joint proposal from the Union Minister for Foreign Affairs and the Commission, shall adopt the necessary European regulations or decisions. It shall inform the European Parliament thereof.

2.   In the areas referred to in paragraph 1, the Council of Ministers may adopt restrictive measures under the same procedure against natural or legal persons and non-State groups or bodies.

Chapter VI   INTERNATIONAL AGREEMENTS

Article III-225

1.   The Union may conclude agreements with one or more third countries or international organisations where the Constitution so provides or where the conclusion of an agreement is necessary in order to achieve, within the framework of the Union's policies, one of the objectives fixed by the Constitution, where there is provision for it in a binding Union legislative act or where it affects one of the Union's internal acts.

2.   Agreements concluded by the Union are binding upon the institutions of the Union and on its Member States.

Article III-226

The Union may conclude association agreements with one or more third countries or international organisations.   Such agreements shall establish an association involving reciprocal rights and obligations, common actions and special procedures.

Article III-227

1.   Without prejudice to the specific provisions laid down in Article III-217, agreements between the Union and third States or international organisations shall be negotiated and concluded in accordance with the following procedure.

2.   The Council of Ministers shall authorise negotiations to be opened, adopt negotiating directives and conclude agreements.

3.   The Commission, or the Union Minister for Foreign Affairs where the agreement exclusively or principally relates to the common foreign and security policy, shall submit recommendations to the Council of Ministers, which shall adopt a European decision authorising the opening of negotiations.

4.   In connection with the European decision authorising negotiation, depending on the subject of the future agreement, the Council of Ministers shall nominate the negotiator or leader of the Union's negotiating team.

5.   The Council of Ministers may address negotiating directives to the Union's negotiator and may designate a special committee in consultation with which the negotiations must be conducted.

6.   On a proposal from the negotiator, the Council of Ministers shall adopt a European decision authorising the signing of the agreement and, if necessary, its provisional application.

7.   The Council of Ministers shall adopt a European decision concluding the agreement on a proposal by the agreement negotiator.

Except where agreements relate exclusively to the common foreign and security policy, the Council of Ministers shall adopt the decision referred to in the first subparagraph after consulting the European Parliament. The European Parliament shall deliver its opinion within a time-limit which the Council of Ministers may lay down according to the urgency of the matter. In the absence of an opinion within that time-limit, the Council of Ministers may act.

The European Parliament's consent shall be required for:

> (a) association agreements;
> (b) Union accession to the European Convention for the Protection of Human Rights and Fundamental Freedoms;
> (c) agreements establishing a specific institutional framework by organising cooperation procedures;
> (d) agreements with important budgetary implications for the Union;
> (e) agreements covering fields to which the legislative procedure applies.

The European Parliament and the Council of Ministers may, in an urgent situation, agree upon a time-limit for consent.

8.   When concluding an agreement, the Council of Ministers may, by way of derogation from paragraphs 6, 7 and 10, authorise the negotiator to approve on the Union's behalf modifications to the agreement where it provides for them to be adopted by a simplified procedure or by a body set up by the agreement; the Council of Ministers may attach specific conditions to such authorisation.

9.   The Council of Ministers shall act by a qualified majority throughout the procedure. It shall act unanimously when the agreement covers a field for which unanimity is required for the adoption of a Union act as well as for association agreements and for Union accession to the European Convention for the Protection of Human Rights and Fundamental Freedoms.

10.   The Council of Ministers, on a proposal from the Union Minister for Foreign Affairs or the Commission, shall adopt a European decision suspending application of an agreement and establishing the positions to be adopted on the Union's behalf in a body set up by an agreement, when that body is called upon to adopt acts having legal effects, with the exception of acts supplementing or amending the institutional framework of the agreement.

11.   The European Parliament shall be immediately and fully informed at all stages of the procedure.

12.   A Member State, the European Parliament, the Council of Ministers or the Commission may obtain the opinion of the Court of Justice as to whether an agreement envisaged is compatible with the provisions of the Constitution. Where the opinion of the Court of Justice is adverse, the agreement envisaged may not enter into force unless it is amended or the Constitution is revised in accordance with the procedure laid down in Article IV-6.

Article III-228

1.   By way of derogation from Article III-227, the Council of Ministers, acting unanimously on a recommendation from the European Central Bank or from the Commission, following consultation with the European Central Bank with a view to reaching a consensus compatible with the objective of price stability and after consultation with the European Parliament, in accordance with the procedure laid down in paragraph 3 for the arrangements there referred to, may conclude formal agreements on a system of exchange rates for the euro in relation to currencies other than those that are legal tender within the Union.

The Council of Ministers, acting by a qualified majority either on a recommendation from the Commission and after consulting the European Central Bank, or on a recommendation from the European Central Bank and in an endeavour to reach a consensus consistent with the objective of price stability, may adopt, adjust or abandon the central rates of the euro within the exchange-rate system. The President of the Council of Ministers shall inform the European Parliament of the adoption, adjustment or abandonment of the central rates of the euro.

2.   In the absence of an exchange-rate system in relation to one or more currencies other than those that are legal tender within the Union as referred to in paragraph 1, the Council of Ministers, acting either on a recommendation from the Commission and after consulting the European Central Bank or on a recommendation from the European Central Bank, may formulate general orientations for exchange-rate policy in relation to these currencies. These general orientations shall be without prejudice to the primary objective of the European System of Central Banks, to maintain price stability.

3.   By way of derogation from Article III-227, where agreements on matters relating to the monetary or exchange-rate system are to be the subject of negotiations between the Union and one or more States or international organisations, the Council of Ministers, acting on a recommendation from the Commission and after consulting the European Central Bank, shall decide the arrangements for the negotiation and for the conclusion of the agreements. These arrangements shall ensure that the Union expresses a single position. The Commission shall be fully associated with the negotiations.

4.   Without prejudice to Union competence and agreements as regards economic and monetary union, Member States may negotiate in international bodies and conclude international agreements.

THE UNION'S RELATIONS WITH INTERNATIONAL ORGANISATIONS AND THIRD COUNTRIES AND UNION DELEGATIONS

Article III-229

1.   The Union shall establish all appropriate forms of cooperation with the United Nations, the Council of Europe, the Organisation for Security and Cooperation in Europe and the Organisation for Economic Cooperation and Development.

2.   It shall also maintain such relations as are appropriate with other international organisations.

3.   The Union Minister for Foreign Affairs and the Commission shall be instructed to implement this Article.

Article III-230

1.   Union delegations in third countries and to international organisations shall represent the Union.

2.   Union delegations shall operate under the authority of the Union Minister for Foreign Affairs and in close cooperation with Member States' diplomatic missions.

Chapter VIII   IMPLEMENTATION OF THE SOLIDARITY CLAUSE

Article III-231

1.   Acting on a joint proposal by the Commission and the Union Minister for Foreign Affairs, the Council of Ministers shall adopt a European decision defining the arrangements for the implementation of the solidarity clause referred to in Article I-42. The European Parliament shall be informed.

2.   Should a Member State fall victim to a terrorist attack or a natural or man-made disaster, the other Member States shall assist it at the request of its political authorities. To that end, the Member States shall coordinate between themselves in the Council of Ministers.

3.   For the purposes of this Article, the Council of Ministers shall be assisted by the Political and Security Committee, with the support of the structures developed in the context of the common security and defence policy, and by the Committee provided for in Article III-162, which shall, if necessary, submit joint opinions.

4.   The European Council shall regularly assess the threats facing the Union in order to enable the Union to take effective action.

THE FUNCTIONING OF THE UNION

Chapter I

PROVISIONS GOVERNING THE INSTITUTIONS

THE INSTITUTIONS

THE EUROPEAN PARLIAMENT

Article III-232

1.   A European law or framework law of the Council of Ministers shall establish the necessary measures for the election of the Members of the European Parliament by direct universal suffrage in accordance with a uniform procedure in all Member States or in accordance with principles common to all Member States.

The Council of Ministers shall act unanimously on a proposal from and after obtaining the consent of the European Parliament, which shall act by a majority of its component members. This law or framework law shall not enter into force until it has been approved by the Member States in accordance with their respective constitutional requirements.

2.   A European law of the European Parliament shall lay down the regulations and general conditions governing the performance of the duties of its Members. The European Parliament shall act on its own initiative after seeking an opinion from the Commission and with the approval of the Council of Ministers. The Council of Ministers shall act unanimously on all rules or conditions relating to the taxation of Members or former Members.

3.   Throughout the 2004-2009 Parliament, the composition of the European Parliament shall be as set out in the Protocol on the representation of citizens in the European Parliament.

Article III-233

A European law shall lay down the regulations governing political parties at European level referred to in Article I-45(4), and in particular the rules regarding their funding.

Article III-234

The European Parliament may, acting by a majority of its component Members, request the Commission to submit any appropriate proposal on matters on which it considers that a Union act is required for the purpose of implementing the Constitution. If the Commission does not submit a proposal, it shall inform the European Parliament of the reasons.

Article III-235

In the course of its duties, the European Parliament may, at the request of a quarter of its component Members, set up a temporary Committee of Inquiry to investigate, without prejudice to the powers conferred by the Constitution on other institutions or bodies, alleged contraventions or maladministration in the implementation of Union law, except where the alleged facts are being examined before a court and while the case is still subject to legal proceedings.

The temporary Committee of Inquiry shall cease to exist on the submission of its report.

A European law of the European Parliament shall lay down the detailed provisions governing the exercise of the right of inquiry. The European Parliament shall act on its own initiative after obtaining the approval of the Council of Ministers and of the Commission.

Article III-236

Any citizen of the Union, and any natural or legal person residing or having its registered office in a Member State, shall have the right to address, individually or in association with other citizens or persons, a petition to the European Parliament on a matter which comes within the Union's fields of activity and which affects him directly.

1.   The European Parliament shall appoint a European Ombudsman. The European Ombudsman shall be empowered to receive complaints from any citizen of the Union or any natural or legal person residing or having its registered office in a Member State concerning instances of maladministration in the activities of the Union's institutions, bodies or agencies, with the exception of the Court of Justice acting in its judicial role.

In accordance with his or her duties, the European Ombudsman shall conduct inquiries for which he or she finds grounds, either on his or her own initiative or on the basis of complaints submitted to him or her direct or through a Member of the European Parliament, except where the alleged facts are or have been the subject of legal proceedings. Where the European Ombudsman establishes an instance of maladministration, he or she shall refer the matter to the institution, body or agency concerned, which shall have a period of three months in which to inform him or her of its views. The European Ombudsman shall then forward a report to the European Parliament and the institution, body or agency concerned. The person lodging the complaint shall be informed of the outcome of such inquiries.

The European Ombudsman shall submit an annual report to the European Parliament on the outcome of his or her inquiries.

2.   The European Ombudsman shall be appointed after each election of the European Parliament for the duration of its term of office. The European Ombudsman shall be eligible for reappointment.

The European Ombudsman may be dismissed by the Court of Justice at the request of the European Parliament if he or she no longer fulfils the conditions required for the performance of his or her duties or if he or she is guilty of serious misconduct.

3.   The European Ombudsman shall be completely independent in the performance of his or her duties. In the performance of those duties he or she shall neither seek nor take instructions from any body. The European Ombudsman may not, during his or her term of office, engage in any other occupation, whether gainful or not.

4.   A European law of the European Parliament shall lay down the regulations and general conditions governing the performance of the European Ombudsman's

duties. The European Parliament shall act on its own initiative after seeking an opinion from the Commission and with the approval of the Council of Ministers.

Article III-238

The European Parliament shall hold an annual session. It shall meet, without requiring to be convened, on the second Tuesday in March.

The European Parliament may meet in extraordinary part-session at the request of a majority of its component Members or at the request of the Council of Ministers or of the Commission.

Article III-239

1.   The Commission may attend all meetings of the European Parliament and shall, at its request, be heard.

The Commission shall reply orally or in writing to questions put to it by the European Parliament or by its Members.

2.   The European Council and the Council of Ministers shall be heard by the European Parliament in accordance with the conditions laid down in the procedural rules of the European Council and the Rules of Procedure of the Council of Ministers.

Article III-240

Save as otherwise provided in the Constitution, the European Parliament shall act by a majority of the votes cast. The Rules of Procedure shall determine the quorum.

Article III-241

The European Parliament shall adopt its Rules of Procedure, acting by a majority of its component Members.

The proceedings of the European Parliament shall be published in the manner laid down in the Constitution and its Rules of Procedure.

Article III-242

The European Parliament shall discuss in open session the annual general report submitted to it by the Commission.

Article III-243

If a motion of censure on the activities of the Commission is tabled before it, the European Parliament shall not vote thereon until at least three days after the motion has been tabled and only by open vote.

If the motion of censure is carried by a two-thirds majority of the votes cast, representing a majority of the component Members of the European Parliament, the Commission shall resign. It shall continue to deal with current business until it is replaced in accordance with Articles I-25 and I-26. In this case, the term of office of the Commission appointed to replace it shall expire on the date on which the term of office of the Commission which was obliged to rcsign would have expired.

Subsection 2   THE EUROPEAN COUNCIL

Article III-244

1.   Where a vote is taken, any member of the European Council may also act on behalf of not more than one other member.

Abstentions by members present in person or represented shall not prevent the adoption by the European Council of decisions which require unanimity.

2.   The President of the European Parliament may be invited to be heard by the European Council.

3.   The European Council shall establish its procedural rules by a simple majority. The European Council shall be assisted by the General Secretariat of the Council of Ministers.

Subsection 3   THE COUNCIL OF MINISTERS

Article III-245

1.   The Council of Ministers shall meet when convened by its President on his or her own initiative, or at the request of one of its members or of the Commission.

2.   The European Council shall adopt by unanimity a European decision establishing the rules governing the rotation of the Presidency of the formations of the Council of Ministers.

Article III-246

1.   Where a vote is taken, any member of the Council of Ministers may also act on behalf of not more than one other member.

2.   Where it is required to act by a simple majority, the Council of Ministers shall act by a majority of its members.

3.   Abstentions by members present in person or represented shall not prevent the adoption by the Council of Ministers of acts which require unanimity.

Article III-247

1.   A committee consisting of the Permanent Representatives of the Member States shall be responsible for preparing the work of the Council of Ministers and for carrying out the tasks assigned to it by the latter. The Committee may adopt procedural decisions in cases provided for in the Rules of Procedure of the Council of Ministers.

2.		The Council of Ministers shall be assisted by a General Secretariat, under the responsibility of a Secretary-General appointed by the Council of Ministers.

The Council of Ministers shall decide on the organisation of the General Secretariat by a simple majority.

3.		The Council of Ministers shall act by a simple majority regarding procedural matters and for the adoption of its Rules of Procedure.

Article III-248

The Council of Ministers, acting by a simple majority, may request the Commission to undertake any studies the Council of Ministers considers desirable for the attainment of the common objectives, and to submit to it any appropriate proposals. If the Commission does not submit a proposal, it shall inform the Council of Ministers of the reasons.

Article III-249

The Council of Ministers shall adopt European decisions laying down the rules governing the committees provided for in the Constitution. It shall act by a simple majority after consulting the Commission.

Subsection 4 THE COMMISSION

Article III-250

European Commissioners and Commissioners shall be appointed for a period of five years, subject, if need be, to Article III-243. Only nationals of Member States may be European Commissioners or Commissioners.

Article III-251

European Commissioners and Commissioners shall refrain from any action incompatible with their duties. Each Member State undertakes to respect this principle and not to seek to influence the European Commissioners and Commissioners in the performance of their tasks.

European Commissioners and Commissioners may not, during their term of office, engage in any other occupation, whether gainful or not. When entering upon their duties they shall give a solemn undertaking that, both during and after their term of office, they will respect the obligations arising therefrom and in particular their duty to behave with integrity and discretion as regards the acceptance, after they have ceased to hold office, of certain appointments or benefits. In the event of any breach of these obligations, the Court of Justice may, on application by the Council of Ministers, acting by a simple majority, or the Commission, rule that the person concerned be, according to the circumstances, either compulsorily retired in accordance with Article III-253 or deprived of his or her right to a pension or other benefits in its stead.

Article III-252

1.   Apart from normal replacement, or death, the duties of a European Commissioner or Commissioner shall end when he or she resigns or is compulsorily retired. A European Commissioner or Commissioner shall resign if the President so requests.

2.   A vacancy caused by resignation, compulsory retirement or death shall be filled for the remainder of the European Commissioner or Commissioner's term of office by a new European Commissioner or Commissioner appointed by the President of the Commission in accordance with Articles I-25 and I-26.

3.   In the event of resignation, compulsory retirement or death, the President shall be replaced for the remainder of his or her term of office in accordance with Article I-26(1).

4.   In the case of the resignation of all European Commissioners and Commissioners, they shall remain in office until they have been replaced, for the remainder of their term of office, in accordance with Articles I-25 and I-26.

Article III-253

If any European Commissioner or Commissioner no longer fulfils the conditions required for the performance of his or her duties or if he or she has been guilty of serious misconduct, the Court of Justice may, on application by the Council of Ministers, acting by a simple majority, or by the Commission, compulsorily retire him or her.

Article III-254

The responsibilities incumbent upon the Commission shall be structured and allocated among its members by its President, in accordance with Article I-26(3) of the Constitution. The President may reshuffle the allocation of those responsibilities during the Commission's term of office. European Commissioners and Commissioners shall carry out the duties devolved upon them by the President under his or her authority.

Article III-255

The Commission shall act by a majority of the members of the College. The Rules of Procedure shall determine the quorum.

Article III-256

The Commission shall adopt its Rules of Procedure so as to ensure both its own operation and that of its departments. It shall ensure that these rules are published.

Article III-257

The Commission shall publish annually, not later than one month before the opening of the session of the European Parliament, a general report on the activities of the Union.

Article III-258

The European Court of Justice shall sit in chambers, as a Grand Chamber or as a full Court, in accordance with the Statute of the Court of Justice.

Article III-259

The European Court of Justice shall be assisted by eight Advocates-General. Should the European Court of Justice so request, the Council of Ministers may, acting unanimously, adopt a European decision to increase the number of Advocates-General.

It shall be the duty of the Advocate-General, acting with complete impartiality and independence, to make, in open court, reasoned submissions on cases which, in accordance with the Statute of the Court of Justice, require his or her involvement.

Article III-260

The Judges and Advocates-General of the European Court of Justice shall be chosen from persons whose independence is beyond doubt and who possess the qualifications required for appointment to the highest judicial offices in their respective countries or who are jurisconsults of recognised competence; they shall be appointed by common accord of the governments of the Member States after consulting the panel provided for in Article III-262.

Every three years there shall be a partial replacement of the Judges and Advocates-General, in accordance with the conditions laid down in the Statute of the Court of Justice.

The Judges shall elect the President of the European Court of Justice from among their number for a term of three years. He or she may be re-elected.

The European Court of Justice shall adopt its Rules of Procedure. Those Rules shall require the approval of the Council of Ministers.

Article III-261

The number of Judges of the High Court shall be determined by the Statute of the Court of Justice. The Statute may provide for the High Court to be assisted by Advocates-General.

The members of the High Court shall be chosen from persons whose independence is beyond doubt and who possess the ability required for appointment to high judicial office. They shall be appointed by common accord of the governments of the Member States after consultation of the panel provided for in Article III-262.

The membership of the High Court shall be partially renewed every three years. Retiring members may be reappointed.

The Judges shall elect the President of the High Court from among their number for a term of three years. He or she may be re-elected.

The High Court shall establish its Rules of Procedure in agreement with the European Court of Justice. The Rules shall be subject to the approval of the Council of Ministers.

Unless the Statute of the Court of Justice provides otherwise, the provisions of the Constitution relating to the European Court of Justice shall apply to the High Court.

Article III-262

A panel shall be set up in order to give an opinion on candidates' suitability to perform the duties of Judge and Advocate-General of the European Court of Justice and the High Court before the governments of the Member States take the decisions referred to in Articles III-260 and III-261.

The panel shall comprise seven persons chosen from among former members of the European Court of Justice and the High Court, members of national supreme courts and lawyers of recognised competence, one of whom shall be proposed by the European Parliament. The Council of Ministers shall adopt a European decision establishing the panel's operating rules and a European decision appointing its members. It shall act on the initiative of the President of the European Court of Justice.

Article III-263

1.   The High Court shall have jurisdiction to hear and determine at first instance actions or proceedings referred to in Articles III-270, III-272, III-275, III-277 and III-279, with the exception of those assigned to a specialised court and those reserved in the Statute for the European Court of Justice. The Statute may provide for the High Court to have jurisdiction for other classes of action or proceeding.

Decisions given by the High Court under this paragraph may be subject to a right of appeal to the European Court of Justice on points of law only, under the conditions and within the limits laid down by the Statute of the Court of Justice.

2.   The High Court shall have jurisdiction to hear and determine actions or proceedings brought against decisions of the specialised courts set up under Article III-264.

Decisions given by the High Court under this paragraph may exceptionally be subject to review by the European Court of Justice, under the conditions and within the limits laid down by the Statute, where there is a serious risk of the unity or consistency of Union law being affected.

3.   The High Court shall have jurisdiction to hear and determine questions referred for a preliminary ruling under Article III-274, in specific areas laid down by the Statute of the Court of Justice.

Where the High Court considers that the case requires a decision of principle likely to affect the unity or consistency of Union law, it may refer the case to the European Court of Justice for a ruling.

Decisions given by the High Court on questions referred for a preliminary ruling may exceptionally be subject to review by the European Court of Justice, under the conditions and within the limits laid down by the Statute, where there is a serious risk of the unity or consistency of Union law being affected.

Article III-264

1.   European laws may establish specialised courts attached to the High Court to hear and determine at first instance certain classes of action or proceeding brought in specific areas. They shall be adopted either on a proposal from the Commission after consultation of the Court of Justice or at the request of the Court of Justice after consultation of the Commission.

2.   The European law establishing a specialised court shall lay down the rules on the organisation of the court and the extent of the jurisdiction conferred upon it.

3.   Decisions given by specialised courts may be subject to a right of appeal on points of law only or, when provided for in the European law establishing the specialised court, a right of appeal also on matters of fact, before the High Court.

4.   The members of the specialised courts shall be chosen from persons whose independence is beyond doubt and who possess the ability required for appointment to judicial office. They shall be appointed by the Council of Ministers, acting unanimously.

5.   The specialised courts shall establish their Rules of Procedure in agreement with the Court of Justice. Those Rules shall require the approval of the Council of Ministers.

6.   Unless the European law establishing the specialised court provides otherwise, the provisions of the Constitution relating to the Court of Justice and the provisions of the Statute of the Court of Justice shall apply to the specialised courts.

Article III-265

If the Commission considers that a Member State has failed to fulfil an obligation under the Constitution, it shall deliver a reasoned opinion on the matter after giving the State concerned the opportunity to submit its observations.

If the State concerned does not comply with the opinion within the period laid down by the Commission, the latter may bring the matter before the Court of Justice.

Article III-266

A Member State which considers that another Member State has failed to fulfil an obligation under the Constitution may bring the matter before the Court of Justice.

Before a Member State brings an action against another Member State for an alleged infringement of an obligation under the Constitution, it shall bring the matter before the Commission.

The Commission shall deliver a reasoned opinion after each of the States concerned has been given the opportunity to submit its own case and its observations on the other party's case both orally and in writing.

If the Commission has not delivered an opinion within three months of the date on which the matter was brought before it, the absence of such opinion shall not prevent the matter from being brought before the Court of Justice.

Article III-267

1.   If the Court of Justice finds that a Member State has failed to fulfil an obligation under the Constitution, the State shall be required to take the necessary measures to comply with the judgment of the Court of Justice.

2.   If the Commission considers that the Member State concerned has not taken the necessary measures to comply with the Court's judgment, it may bring the case before the Court of Justice after giving that State the opportunity to submit its observations. It shall specify the amount of the lump sum or penalty payment to be paid by the Member State concerned which it considers appropriate in the circumstances.

If the Court of Justice finds that the Member State concerned has not complied with its judgment it may impose a lump sum or penalty payment on it.

This procedure shall be without prejudice to Article III-266.

3.   When the Commission brings a case before the Court of Justice pursuant to Article III-265 on the grounds that the State concerned has failed to fulfil its obligations to notify measures transposing a European framework law, it may, when it deems appropriate, request that, in the course of the same proceedings, the Court of Justice impose the payment of a lump sum or penalty payment if the Court finds that there has been such a failure. If the Court of Justice complies with the Commission's request, the payment in question shall take effect within the time limit laid down by the Court of Justice in its judgment.

Article III-268

European laws and European regulations of the Council of Ministers may give the Court of Justice unlimited jurisdiction with regard to the penalties provided for in them.

Article III-269

Without prejudice to the other provisions of the Constitution, a European law may confer on the Court of Justice, to the extent that it shall determine, jurisdiction in disputes relating to the application of acts adopted on the basis of the Constitution which create European intellectual property rights.

Article III-270

1.   The Court of Justice shall review the legality of European laws and framework laws, of acts of the Council of Ministers, of the Commission and of the European Central Bank, other than recommendations and opinions, and of acts of the European Parliament intended to produce legal effects vis-à-vis third parties. It shall also review the legality of acts of bodies or agencies of the Union intended to produce legal effects vis-à-vis third parties.

2.   It shall for this purpose have jurisdiction in actions brought by a Member State, the European Parliament, the Council of Ministers or the Commission on grounds of lack of competence, infringement of an essential procedural requirement, infringement of the Constitution or of any rule of law relating to its application, or misuse of powers.

3.   The Court of Justice shall have jurisdiction under the same conditions in actions brought by the Court of Auditors, by the European Central Bank and by the Committee of the Regions for the purpose of protecting their prerogatives.

4.　　　　Any natural or legal person may, under the same conditions, institute proceedings against an act addressed to that person or which is of direct and individual concern to him or her, and against a regulatory act which is of direct concern to him or her and does not entail implementing measures.

5.　　　　Acts setting up bodies and agencies of the Union may lay down specific conditions and arrangements concerning actions brought by natural or legal persons against acts of these bodies or agencies intended to produce legal effects.

6.　　　　The proceedings provided for in this Article shall be instituted within two months of the publication of the act, or of its notification to the plaintiff, or, in the absence thereof, of the day on which it came to the knowledge of the latter, as the case may be.

Article III-271

If the action is well founded the Court of Justice shall declare the act concerned to be void.

However, the Court of Justice shall, if it considers this necessary, state which of the effects of the act which it has declared void shall be considered as definitive.

Article III-272

Should the European Parliament, the Council of Ministers, the Commission or the European Central Bank, in infringement of the Constitution, fail to act, the Member States and the other Institutions of the Union may bring an action before the Court of Justice to have the infringement established. This provision shall apply, under the same conditions, to bodies and agencies of the Union which fail to act.

The action shall be admissible only if the Institution, body or agency concerned has first been called upon to act. If, within two months of being so called upon, the Institution, agency or body concerned has not defined its position, the action may be brought within a further period of two months.

Any natural or legal person may, under the conditions laid down in the preceding paragraphs, complain to the Court of Justice that an Institution, body or agency of the Union has failed to address to that person any act other than a recommendation or an opinion.

Article III-273

The Institution or Institutions, body or agency whose act has been declared void, or whose failure to act has been declared contrary to the Constitution, shall be required to take the necessary measures to comply with the judgment of the Court of Justice.

This obligation shall not affect any obligation which may result from the application of the second paragraph of Article III-337.

Article III-274

The Court of Justice shall have jurisdiction to give preliminary rulings concerning:

       (a) the interpretation of the Constitution;
       (b) the validity and interpretation of acts of the Institutions of the Union.

Where such a question is raised before any court or tribunal of a Member State, that court or tribunal may, if it considers that a decision on the question is necessary to enable it to give judgment, request the Court of Justice to give a ruling thereon.

Where any such question is raised in a case pending before a court or tribunal of a Member State against whose decisions there is no judicial remedy under national law, that court or tribunal shall bring the matter before the Court of Justice.

If such a question is raised in a case pending before a court or tribunal of a Member State with regard to a person in custody, the Court of Justice shall act with the minimum of delay.

Article III-275

The Court of Justice shall have jurisdiction in disputes relating to compensation for damage provided for in the second paragraph of Article III-337.

Article III-276

At the request of the Member State concerned by a determination made by the European Council or the Council of Ministers pursuant to Article I-58, the European Court of Justice shall have jurisdiction solely on the procedural stipulations contained in that Article. The Court shall rule within one month from the date of that determination.

Article III-277

The Court of Justice shall have jurisdiction in any dispute between the Union and its servants within the limits and under the conditions laid down in the Staff Regulations of Officials and the Conditions of Employment of other servants of the Union.

Article III-278

The Court of Justice shall, within the limits hereinafter laid down, have jurisdiction in disputes concerning:

(a) the fulfilment by Member States of obligations under the Statute of the European Investment Bank. In this connection, the Board of Directors of the Bank shall enjoy the powers conferred upon the Commission by Article III-265;

(b) measures adopted by the Board of Governors of the European Investment Bank. In this connection, any Member State, the Commission or the Board of Directors of the Bank may institute proceedings under the conditions laid down in Article III-270;

(c) measures adopted by the Board of Directors of the European Investment Bank. Proceedings against such measures may be instituted only by Member States or by the Commission, under the conditions laid down in Article III-270, and solely on the grounds of non-compliance with the procedure provided for in Article 21(2), (5), (6) and (7) of the Statute of the Bank;

(d) the fulfilment by national central banks of obligations under the Constitution and the Statute of the European System of Central Banks and the European Central Bank. In this connection, the powers of the Council of the European Central Bank in respect of national central banks shall be the same as those conferred upon the Commission in respect of Member States by Article III-265. If the Court of Justice finds that a national central bank has failed to fulfil an obligation under the Constitution, that bank shall be required to take the necessary measures to comply with the judgment of the Court of Justice.

Article III-279

The Court of Justice shall have jurisdiction to give judgment pursuant to any arbitration clause contained in a contract concluded by or on behalf of the Union, whether that contract be governed by public or private law.

Article III-280

The Court of Justice shall have jurisdiction in any dispute between Member States which relates to the subject matter of the Constitution if the dispute is submitted to it under a special agreement between the parties.

Article III-281

Save where jurisdiction is conferred on the Court of Justice by the Constitution, disputes to which the Union is a party shall not on that ground be excluded from the jurisdiction of the courts or tribunals of the Member States.

Article III-282

The Court of Justice shall not have jurisdiction with respect to Articles I-39 and I-40 and the provisions of Chapter II of Title V of Part III concerning the common foreign and security policy.

However, the Court of Justice shall have jurisdiction to rule on proceedings reviewing the legality of restrictive measures against natural or legal persons, adopted by the Council on the basis of Article III-224, and brought in accordance with the conditions laid down in Article III-270(4).

Article III-283

In exercising its competences regarding the provisions of Sections 4 and 5 of Chapter IV of Title III concerning the area of freedom, security and justice, the Court of Justice shall have no jurisdiction to review the validity or proportionality of operations carried out by the police or other law-enforcement services of a Member State or the exercise of the responsibilities incumbent upon Member States with regard to the maintenance of law and order and the safeguarding of internal security, where such action is a matter of national law.

Article III-284

Member States undertake not to submit a dispute concerning the interpretation or application of the Constitution to any method of settlement other than those provided for therein.

Article III-285

Notwithstanding the expiry of the period laid down in Article III-270(6), any party may, in proceedings in which a European law or a European regulation of the Council of Ministers, of the Commission, or of the European Central Bank is at issue, plead the grounds specified in Article III-270(2) in order to invoke before the Court of Justice the inapplicability of that act.

Article III-286

Actions brought before the Court of Justice shall not have suspensory effect. The Court of Justice may, however, if it considers that circumstances so require, order that application of the contested act be suspended.

Article III-287

The Court of Justice may in any cases before it prescribe any necessary interim measures.

Article III-288

The judgments of the Court of Justice shall be enforceable under the conditions laid down in Article III-307.

Article III-289

The Statute of the Court of Justice shall be laid down in a Protocol.

A European law may amend the provisions of the Statute, with the exception of Title I and Article 64. It shall be adopted either at the request of the Court of Justice and after consultation of the Commission, or on a proposal from the Commission and after consultation of the Court of Justice.

Subsection 6   THE COURT OF AUDITORS

Article III-290

1.   The Court of Auditors shall examine the accounts of all revenue and expenditure of the Union. It shall also examine the accounts of all revenue and expenditure of all bodies set up by the Union insofar as the relevant constituent instrument does not preclude such examination.

The Court of Auditors shall provide the European Parliament and the Council of Ministers with a statement of assurance as to the reliability of the accounts and the legality and regularity of the underlying transactions which shall be published in the *Official Journal of the European Union*. This statement may be supplemented by specific assessments for each major area of Union activity.

2.   The Court of Auditors shall examine whether all revenue has been received and all expenditure incurred in a lawful and regular manner and whether the financial management has been sound. In doing so, it shall report in particular on any cases of irregularity.

The audit of revenue shall be carried out on the basis both of the amounts established as due and the amounts actually paid to the Union.

The audit of expenditure shall be carried out on the basis both of commitments undertaken and payments made.

These audits may be carried out before the closure of accounts for the financial year in question.

3.   The audit shall be based on records and, if necessary, performed on the spot in the other Institutions, on the premises of any body which manages revenue or expenditure on behalf of the Union and in the Member States, including on the premises of any natural or legal person in receipt of payments from the budget. In the Member States the audit shall be carried out in liaison with national audit bodies or, if these do not have the necessary powers, with the competent national departments. The Court of Auditors and the national audit bodies of the Member States shall cooperate in a spirit of trust while maintaining their independence. These bodies or departments shall inform the Court of Auditors whether they intend to take part in the audit.

The other Institutions, any bodies managing revenue or expenditure on behalf of the Union, any natural or legal person in receipt of payments from the budget, and the national audit bodies or, if these do not have the necessary powers, the competent national departments, shall forward to the Court of Auditors, at its request, any document or information necessary to carry out its task.

In respect of the European Investment Bank's activity in managing Union expenditure and revenue, rights of access by the Court of Auditors to information held by the Bank shall be governed by an agreement between the Court, the Bank and the Commission. In the absence of an agreement, the Court shall nevertheless have access to information necessary for the audit of Union expenditure and revenue managed by the Bank.

4.   The Court of Auditors shall draw up an annual report after the close of each financial year. It shall be forwarded to the other Institutions and shall be published, together with the replies of these Institutions to the observations of the Court of Auditors, in the *Official Journal of the European Union.*

The Court of Auditors may also, at any time, submit observations, particularly in the form of special reports, on specific questions and deliver opinions at the request of one of the other Institutions.

It shall adopt its annual reports, special reports or opinions by a majority of its Members. However, it may establish internal chambers in order to adopt certain categories of reports or opinions under the conditions laid down by its Rules of Procedure.

It shall assist the European Parliament and the Council of Ministers in exercising their powers of control over the implementation of the budget.

The Court of Auditors shall adopt its Rules of Procedure. Those rules shall require the approval of the Council of Ministers.

Article III-291

1.   The Members of the Court of Auditors shall be chosen from among persons who belong or have belonged in their respective countries to external audit bodies or who are especially qualified for this office. Their independence must be beyond doubt.

2.   The Members of the Court of Auditors shall be appointed for a term of six years. Their term of office shall be renewable. The Council of Ministers shall adopt a European decision establishing the list of Members drawn up in accordance with the proposals made by each Member State. It shall act after consulting the European Parliament.

The Members of the Court of Auditors shall elect their President from among their number for a term of three years. He or she may be re-elected.

3.   The Members of the Court of Auditors shall, in the Union's general interest, be completely independent in the performance of their duties.

In the performance of these duties, they shall neither seek nor take instructions from any government or from any other body. They shall refrain from any action incompatible with their duties.

4.   The Members of the Court of Auditors may not, during their term of office, engage in any other occupation, whether gainful or not. When entering upon their duties they shall give a solemn undertaking that, both during and after their term of office, they will respect the obligations arising therefrom and in particular their duty to behave with integrity and discretion as regards the acceptance, after they have ceased to hold office, of certain appointments or benefits.

5. Apart from normal replacement, or death, the duties of a Member of the Court of Auditors shall end when he or she resigns, or is compulsorily retired by a ruling of the Court of Justice pursuant to paragraph 6.

The vacancy thus caused shall be filled for the remainder of the Member's term of office.

Save in the case of compulsory retirement, Members of the Court of Auditors shall remain in office until they have been replaced.

6. A Member of the Court of Auditors may be deprived of his or her office or of his or her right to a pension or other benefits in its stead only if the Court of Justice, at the request of the Court of Auditors, finds that he or she no longer fulfils the requisite conditions or meets the obligations arising from his or her office.

Section 2   THE UNION'S ADVISORY BODIES

Subsection 1   THE COMMITTEE OF THE REGIONS

Article III-292

The number of members of the Committee of the Regions shall not exceed 350. The Council of Ministers shall unanimously adopt a European decision determining the Committee's composition.

The members of the Committee and an equal number of alternate members shall be appointed for five years. Their term of office shall be renewable.

The Council of Ministers shall adopt the European decision establishing the list of members and alternate members drawn up in accordance with the proposals made by each Member State.

When the mandate referred to in Article I-31(2) on the basis of which they were proposed comes to an end, the term of office of members of the Committee shall terminate automatically and they shall then be replaced for the remainder of the said term of office in accordance with the same procedure.

No member of the Committee shall at the same time be a Member of the European Parliament.

Article III-293

The Committee of the Regions shall elect its chairman and officers from among its members for a term of two and a half years.

It shall adopt its Rules of Procedure.

The Committee shall be convened by its chairman at the request of the European Parliament, of the Council of Ministers or of the Commission. It may also meet on its own initiative.

Article III-294

The Committee of the Regions shall be consulted by the European Parliament, by the Council of Ministers or by the Commission where the Constitution so provides and in all other cases, in particular those which concern cross-border cooperation, in which one of these Institutions considers it appropriate.

The European Parliament, the Council of Ministers or the Commission shall, if it considers it necessary, set the Committee, for the submission of its opinion, a time-limit which may not be less than one month from the date on which the chairman receives notification to this effect. Upon expiry of the time-limit, the absence of an opinion shall not prevent further action.

Where the Economic and Social Committee is consulted pursuant to Article III-298, the Committee of the Regions shall be informed by the European Parliament, the Council of Ministers or the Commission of the request for an opinion. It may issue an opinion on its own initiative in cases in which it considers such action appropriate.

The opinion of the Committee, together with a record of the proceedings, shall be forwarded to the European Parliament, to the Council of Ministers and to the Commission.

Article III-295

The number of members of the Economic and Social Committee shall not exceed 350. The Council of Ministers shall unanimously adopt a European decision determining the Committee's composition.

Article III-296

The members of the Economic and Social Committee shall be appointed for five years. Their term of office shall be renewable. The Council of Ministers shall adopt the European decision establishing the list of members drawn up in accordance with the proposals made by each Member State.

The Council of Ministers shall act after consulting the Commission. It may obtain the opinion of European bodies which are representative of the various economic and social sectors and of civil society to which the Union's activities are of concern.

Article III-297

The Economic and Social Committee shall elect its chairman and officers from among its members for a term of two and a half years.

It shall adopt its Rules of Procedure.

It shall be convened by its chairman at the request of the European Parliament, of the Council of Ministers or of the Commission. It may also meet on its own initiative.

Article III-298

The Economic and Social Committee must be consulted by the European Parliament, by the Council of Ministers or by the Commission where the Constitution so provides. In all other cases, it may be consulted by these Institutions. It may also issue an opinion on its own initiative.

The European Parliament, the Council of Ministers or the Commission shall, if it considers it necessary, set the Committee, for the submission of its opinion, a time-limit which may not be less than one month from the date on which the chairman receives notification to this effect. Upon expiry of the time-limit, the absence of an opinion shall not prevent further action.

The opinion of the Committee together with a record of the proceedings shall be forwarded to the European Parliament, to the Council of Ministers and to the Commission.

Section 3   THE EUROPEAN INVESTMENT BANK

Article III-299

The European Investment Bank shall have legal personality.

The members of the European Investment Bank shall be the Member States.

The Statute of the European Investment Bank is laid down in a Protocol. European laws may amend Articles 4, 11 and 12 and Article 18(5) of the Statute of the Bank, either at the request of the European Investment Bank and after consultation of the Commission, or on a proposal from the Commission and after consultation of the European Investment Bank.

Article III-300

The task of the European Investment Bank shall be to contribute, by having recourse to the capital market and utilising its own resources, to the balanced and steady development of the internal market in the Union's interest. For this purpose the Bank shall, operating on a non-profit-making basis, grant loans and give guarantees which facilitate the financing of the following projects in all sectors of the economy:

(a) projects for developing less-developed regions;
(b) projects for modernising or converting undertakings or for developing

fresh activities called for by the progressive establishment of the internal market, where these projects are of such a size or nature that they cannot be entirely financed by the various means available in the individual Member States;

(c) projects of common interest to several Member States which are of such a size or nature that they cannot be entirely financed by the various means available in the individual Member States.

In carrying out its task, the Bank shall facilitate the financing of investment programmes in conjunction with assistance from the Structural Funds and other Union financial instruments.

Section 4   PROVISIONS COMMON TO UNION INSTITUTIONS, BODIES AND AGENCIES

Article III-301

1.   Where, pursuant to the Constitution, the Council of Ministers acts on a proposal from the Commission, unanimity shall be required for an act constituting an amendment to that proposal, subject to Articles I-54, III-302(10) and (13), and III-310.

2.   As long as the Council of Ministers has not acted, the Commission may alter its proposal at any time during the procedures leading to the adoption of a Union act.

Article III-302

1.   Where, pursuant to the Constitution, European laws or framework laws are adopted under the ordinary legislative procedure the following provisions shall apply.

2.   The Commission shall submit a proposal to the European Parliament and the Council of Ministers.

3.   The European Parliament shall adopt its position at first reading and communicate it to the Council of Ministers.

4.   If the Council of Ministers approves the European Parliament's position, the proposed act shall be adopted.

5.   If the Council of Ministers does not approve the European Parliament's position, it shall adopt its position at first reading and communicate it to the European Parliament.

6.   The Council of Ministers shall inform the European Parliament fully of the reasons which led it to adopt its position at first reading. The Commission shall inform the European Parliament fully of its position.

Second reading

7.   If, within three months of such communication, the European Parliament

(a) approves the position of the Council of Ministers at first reading or has not taken a decision, the proposed act shall be deemed to have been adopted;

(b) rejects, by a majority of its component members, the position of the Council of Ministers at first reading, the proposed act shall be deemed not to have been adopted;

(c) proposes, by a majority of its component members, amendments to the position of the Council of Ministers at first reading, the text thus amended shall be forwarded to the Council of Ministers and to the Commission, which shall deliver an opinion on those amendments.

8.   If, within three months of receiving the European Parliament's amendments, the Council of Ministers, acting by a qualified majority,

(a) approves all those amendments, the act in question shall be deemed to have been adopted;

(b) does not approve all the amendments, the President of the Council of Ministers, in agreement with the President of the European Parliament, shall within six weeks convene a meeting of the Conciliation Committee.

9.   The Council of Ministers shall act unanimously on the amendments on which the Commission has delivered a negative opinion.

Conciliation

10.   The Conciliation Committee, which shall be composed of the members of the Council of Ministers or their representatives and an equal number of members representing the European Parliament, shall have the task of reaching agreement on a joint text, by a qualified majority of the members of the Council of Ministers or their representatives and by a majority of the members representing the European Parliament within six weeks of its being convened, on the basis of the positions of the Parliament and the Council of Ministers at second reading.

11.   The Commission shall take part in the Conciliation Committee's proceedings and shall take all the necessary initiatives with a view to reconciling the positions of the European Parliament and the Council of Ministers.

12.   If, within six weeks of its being convened, the Conciliation Committee does not approve the joint text, the proposed act shall be deemed not to have been adopted.

Third reading

13.   If, within that period, the Conciliation Committee approves a joint text, the European Parliament, acting by a majority of the votes cast, and the Council of Ministers, acting by a qualified majority, shall each have a period of six weeks from that date in which to adopt the act in question in accordance with the joint text. If they fail to do so, the proposed act shall be deemed not to have been adopted.

14.   The periods of three months and six weeks referred to in this Article shall be extended by a maximum of one month and two weeks respectively at the initiative of the European Parliament or the Council of Ministers.

Special provisions

15.   Where, in the cases specifically provided for in the Constitution, a law or framework law is submitted to the ordinary legislative procedure on the initiative of a group of Member States, on a recommendation by the European Central Bank, or at the request of the Court of Justice or the European Investment Bank, paragraph 2, the second sentence of paragraph 6, and paragraph 9 shall not apply.

The European Parliament and the Council of Ministers shall communicate the proposed act to the Commission with their positions at first and second readings.

The European Parliament or the Council of Ministers may request the opinion of the Commission throughout the procedure. The Commission also may deliver an opinion on its own initiative. It may, if it deems it necessary, take part in the Conciliation Committee on the terms laid down in paragraph 11.

Article III-303

The European Parliament, the Council of Ministers and the Commission shall consult each other and by common agreement make arrangements for their cooperation. To that end, they may, in compliance with the Constitution, conclude interinstitutional agreements which may be of a binding nature.

Article III-304

1.   In carrying out their missions, the Institutions, bodies and agencies of the Union shall have the support of an open, efficient and independent European administration.

2.   Without prejudice to Article III-332, European laws shall establish specific provisions to that end.

Article III-305

1.   The Institutions, bodies and agencies of the Union shall recognise the importance of transparency in their work and shall, in application of Article I-49, lay down in their rules of procedure the specific provisions for public access to documents. The Court of Justice and the European Central Bank shall be subject to the provisions of Article I-49(3) when exercising their administrative tasks.

2.   The European Parliament and the Council of Ministers shall ensure publication of the documents relating to the legislative procedures.

Article III-306

1.   The Council of Ministers shall adopt European regulations and decisions determining:

> (a) the salaries, allowances and pensions of the President of the European Council, the President of the Commission, the Union Minister for Foreign Affairs, the European Commissioners and Commissioners, the President, Members and Registrar of the European Court of Justice and the Members and Registrar of the High Court;
>
> (b) the conditions of employment, in particular the salaries, allowances and pensions, of the President and Members of the Court of Auditors.

It shall also determine any payment to be made instead of remuneration.

2.   The Council of Ministers shall adopt European regulations and decisions determining the allowances of the Members of the Economic and Social Committee.

Article III-307

Acts of the Council of Ministers, of the Commission or of the European Central Bank which impose a pecuniary obligation on persons other than States shall be enforceable.

Enforcement shall be governed by the rules of civil procedure in force in the Member State in the territory of which it is carried out. The order for its enforcement shall be appended to the decision, without other formality than verification of the authenticity of the decision, by the national authority which the government of each Member State shall designate for this purpose and shall make known to the Commission and the Court of Justice.

When these formalities have been completed on application by the party concerned, the latter may proceed to enforcement by bringing the matter directly before the competent authority in accordance with the national law.

Enforcement may be suspended only by a decision of the Court of Justice. However, the courts of the country concerned shall have jurisdiction over complaints that enforcement is being carried out in an irregular manner.

Chapter II — FINANCIAL PROVISIONS

Chapter II **FINANCIAL PROVISIONS**

Section 1 — THE MULTIANNUAL FINANCIAL FRAMEWORK

Section 1 **THE MULTIANNUAL FINANCIAL FRAMEWORK**

Article III-308

1.   The multiannual financial framework shall be established for a period of at least five years in accordance with Article I-54.

2.   The financial framework shall fix the amounts of the annual ceilings on commitment appropriations by category of expenditure and of the annual ceiling on payment appropriations. The categories of expenditure, few in number, shall correspond to the Union's major sectors of activity.

3.   The financial framework shall lay down any other provisions required for the annual budgetary procedure to run smoothly.

4.   Where no European law of the Council of Ministers establishing a new financial framework has been adopted by the end of the previous financial framework, the ceilings and other provisions corresponding to the last year of that framework shall be extended until such time as that law is adopted.

5.   Throughout the procedure leading to the adoption of the financial framework, the European Parliament, the Council of Ministers and the Commission shall take any measure necessary to facilitate the successful completion of the procedure.

Section 2 — THE UNION'S ANNUAL BUDGET

Section 2 **THE UNION'S ANNUAL BUDGET**

Article III-309

The financial year shall run from 1 January to 31 December.

Article III-310

European laws shall establish the Union's annual budget in accordance with the following provisions:

1.   Each Institution shall, before 1 July, draw up estimates of its expenditure. The Commission shall consolidate these estimates in a draft budget. It shall attach thereto an opinion which may contain different estimates.

The draft budget shall contain an estimate of revenue and an estimate of expenditure.

The Commission may amend the draft budget during the procedure until such time as the Conciliation Committee, referred to in paragraph 5 below, is convened.

2.   The Commission shall submit the draft budget to the European Parliament and to the Council of Ministers not later than 1 September of the year preceding that in which the budget is to be implemented.

3.   The Council of Ministers shall adopt its position on the draft budget and forward it to the European Parliament not later than 1 October of the year preceding that in which the budget is to be implemented. The Council of Ministers shall inform the European Parliament fully of the reasons which led it to adopt its position.

4.   If, within forty-two days of such communication, the European Parliament:

   (a) approves the position of the Council of Ministers or has not taken a decision, the European budget law shall be deemed to have been adopted;
   (b) proposes amendments to the position of the Council of Ministers by a majority of its component members, the amended text shall be forwarded to the Council of Ministers and to the Commission. The President of the European Parliament, in agreement with the President of the Council of Ministers, shall immediately convene a meeting of the Conciliation Committee.

If, within ten days, the Council of Ministers informs the European Parliament that it has approved all its amendments, the Conciliation Committee shall not meet.

5.   The Conciliation Committee, which shall be composed of the members of the Council of Ministers or their representatives and an equal number of members rep-

resenting the European Parliament, shall have the task of reaching agreement on a joint text, by a qualified majority of the members of the Council of Ministers or their representatives and by a majority of the members representing the European Parliament within twenty-one days of its being convened, on the basis of the positions of the European Parliament and the Council of Ministers.

6.   The Commission shall take part in the Conciliation Committee's proceedings and shall take all the necessary initiatives with a view to reconciling the positions of the European Parliament and the Council of Ministers.

7.   If, within the twenty-one days referred to in paragraph 5, the Conciliation Committee approves a joint text, the European Parliament, acting by a majority of the votes cast, and the Council of Ministers, acting by a qualified majority, shall each have a period of fourteen days from that date in which to adopt the joint text.

8.   If, within the twenty-one days referred to in paragraph 5, the Conciliation Committee does not approve a joint text or if the Council of Ministers rejects the joint text, the Parliament may, within fourteen days, acting by a majority of its component members and three fifths of the votes cast, confirm its amendments. Where the Parliament amendment is not confirmed, the position of the Council of Ministers on the budget item which is the subject of the amendment shall be deemed to be adopted.

However, if the Parliament, acting by a majority of its component members and three fifths of the votes cast, rejects the joint text, it may ask for a new draft budget to be submitted.

9.   When the procedure provided for in this Article has been completed, the President of the European Parliament shall declare that the European budget law has been finally adopted.

Article III-311

1.   If no European budget law has been adopted at the beginning of a financial year, a sum equivalent to not more than one twelfth of the budget appropriations entered in the European budget law for the preceding financial year may be spent each month in respect of any chapter or other subdivision of the budget in accordance with the provisions of the European law referred to in Article III-318; this arrangement shall not, how-

ever, have the effect of placing at the disposal of the Commission appropriations in excess of one twelfth of those provided for in the draft budget under consideration.

2.   The Council of Ministers, on a proposal by the Commission and in compliance with the other conditions laid down in paragraph 1, may adopt a European decision authorising expenditure in excess of one twelfth. The Council of Ministers shall forward the decision immediately to the European Parliament.

The European decision shall lay down the necessary measures relating to resources to ensure application of this Article.

It shall enter into force thirty days following its adoption if the European Parliament, acting by a majority of its component members, has not decided to reduce this expenditure within that time-limit.

Article III-312

In accordance with the conditions laid down by the European law referred to in Article III-318, any appropriations, other than those relating to staff expenditure, that are unexpended at the end of the financial year may be carried forward to the next financial year only.

Appropriations shall be classified under different chapters grouping items of expenditure according to their nature or purpose and subdivided in accordance with the European law referred to in Article III-318.

The expenditure of the European Parliament, the Council of Ministers, the Commission and the Court of Justice shall be set out in separate parts of the budget, without prejudice to special arrangements for certain common items of expenditure.

IMPLEMENTATION OF
THE BUDGET AND DISCHARGE

Article III-313

The Commission shall implement the budget in cooperation with the Member States, in accordance with the European law referred to in Article III-318, on its own responsibility and within the limits of the appropriations allocated, having regard to the principles of sound financial management. Member States shall cooperate with the Commission to ensure that the appropriations are used in accordance with those principles.

The European law referred to in Article III-318 shall establish the control and audit obligations of the Member States in the implementation of the budget and the resulting responsibilities.

The European law referred to in Article III-318 shall establish the responsibilities and detailed rules for each Institution concerning its part in effecting its own expenditure.

The Commission may, subject to the limits and conditions laid down by the European law referred to in Article III-318, make transfers of appropriations between chapters or between subdivisions within the budget.

Article III-314

The Commission shall submit annually to the European Parliament and to the Council of Ministers the accounts of the preceding financial year relating to the implementation of the budget. The Commission shall also forward to them a financial statement of the Union's assets and liabilities.

The Commission shall also submit to the European Parliament and to the Council of Ministers an evaluation report on the Union's finances based on the results achieved, in particular in relation to the indications given by the European Parliament and the Council of Ministers pursuant to Article III-315.

Article III-315

1.   The European Parliament, on a recommendation from the Council of Ministers, shall give a discharge to the Commission in respect of the implementation of the budget. To this end, the Council of Ministers and the European Parliament in turn shall examine the accounts, the financial statement and the evaluation report referred to in Article III-314, the annual report by the Court of Auditors together with the replies of the Institutions under audit to the observations of the Court of Auditors, the statement of assurance referred to in the second subparagraph of Article III-290(1) and any relevant special reports by the Court of Auditors.

2.   Before giving a discharge to the Commission, or for any other purpose in connection with the exercise of its powers over the implementation of the budget, the European Parliament may ask to hear the Commission give evidence with regard to the execution of expenditure or the operation of financial control systems. The Commission shall submit any necessary information to the European Parliament at the latter's request.

3.   The Commission shall take all appropriate steps to act on the observations in the decisions giving discharge and on other observations by the European Parliament relating to the execution of expenditure, as well as on comments accompanying the recommendations on discharge adopted by the Council of Ministers.

4.   At the request of the European Parliament or the Council of Ministers, the Commission shall report on the measures taken in the light of these observations and comments and in particular on the instructions given to the departments which are responsible for the implementation of the budget. These reports shall also be forwarded to the Court of Auditors.

Section 4   COMMON PROVISIONS

Article III-316

The multiannual financial framework and the annual budget shall be drawn up in euro.

Article III-317

The Commission may, provided it notifies the competent authorities of the Member States concerned, transfer into the currency of one of the Member States its holdings in the currency of another Member State, to the extent necessary to enable them to be used for purposes which come within the scope of the Constitution. The Commission shall as far as possible avoid making such transfers if it possesses cash or liquid assets in the currencies which it needs.

The Commission shall deal with each Member State concerned through the authority designated by that State. In carrying out financial operations the Commission shall employ the services of the bank of issue of the Member State concerned or of any other financial institution approved by that State.

Article III-318

1. European laws shall:

    (a) lay down the financial rules which determine in particular the procedure to be adopted for establishing and implementing the budget and for presenting and auditing accounts;
    (b) lay down rules concerning the responsibility of financial controllers, authorising officers and accounting officers.

They shall be adopted after consultation of the Court of Auditors.

2. The Council of Ministers shall, on a proposal from the Commission, adopt a European regulation laying down the methods and procedure whereby the budget revenue provided under the arrangements relating to the Union's own resources shall be made available to the Commission, and the measures to be applied, if need be, to meet cash requirements. The Council of Ministers shall act after consulting the European Parliament and the Court of Auditors.

3. The Council of Ministers shall act unanimously until 1 January 2007 in all the cases referred to by this Article.

Article III-319

The European Parliament, the Council of Ministers and the Commission shall ensure that the financial means are made available to allow the Union to fulfil its legal obligations in respect of third parties.

Article III-320

Regular meetings between the Presidents of the European Parliament, the Council of Ministers and the Commission shall be convened on the initiative of the Commission under the budgetary procedures referred to in this Chapter. The Presidents shall take all the necessary steps to promote consultation and the reconciliation of the Institutions' positions to facilitate the implementation of the provisions of this Chapter.

Section 5   COMBATING FRAUD

Article III-321

1.   The Union and the Member States shall counter fraud and any other illegal activities affecting the Union's financial interests through measures adopted in accordance with this Article. These measures shall act as a deterrent and be such as to afford effective protection in the Member States.

2.   Member States shall take the same steps to counter fraud affecting the Union's financial interests as they take to counter fraud affecting their own financial interests.

3.   Without prejudice to other provisions of the Constitution, the Member States shall coordinate their action aimed at protecting the Union's financial interests against fraud. To this end they shall organise, together with the Commission, close and regular cooperation between the competent authorities.

4.   European laws or framework laws shall lay down the necessary measures in the fields of the prevention of and fight against fraud affecting the Union's financial interests with a view to affording effective and equivalent protection in the Member States. They shall be adopted after consultation of the Court of Auditors.

5.   The Commission, in cooperation with Member States, shall each year submit to the European Parliament and to the Council of Ministers a report on the measures and provisions adopted for the implementation of this Article.

Chapter III   ENHANCED COOPERATION

Article III-322

Any enhanced cooperation proposed shall comply with the Union's Constitution and law.

Such cooperation shall not undermine the internal market or economic, social and territorial cohesion. It shall not constitute a barrier to or discrimination in trade between Member States, nor shall it distort competition between them.

Article III-323

Any enhanced cooperation proposed shall respect the competences, rights and obligations of those Member States which do not participate in it. Those Member States shall not impede its implementation by the participating Member States.

Article III-324

1.   When enhanced cooperation is being established, it shall be open to all Member States, subject to compliance with any conditions of participation laid down by the European authorising decision. It shall also be open to them at any other time, subject to compliance with the acts already adopted within that framework, in addition to any such conditions.

The Commission and the Member States participating in enhanced cooperation shall ensure that they facilitate participation by as many Member States as possible.

2.   The Commission and, where appropriate, the Union Minister for Foreign Affairs shall keep all members of the Council of Ministers and the European Parliament regularly informed regarding developments in enhanced cooperation.

Article III-325

1.   Member States which wish to establish enhanced cooperation between themselves in one of the areas covered by the Constitution, with the exception of the com-

mon foreign and security policy, shall address a request to the Commission, specifying the scope and objectives of the enhanced cooperation proposed. The Commission may submit a proposal to the Council of Ministers to that effect. In the event of the Commission not submitting a proposal, it shall inform the Member States concerned of the reasons for not doing so.

Authorisation to proceed with enhanced cooperation shall be granted by a European decision of the Council of Ministers, acting on a proposal from the Commission and after obtaining the consent of the European Parliament.

2.   In the framework of the common foreign and security policy, the request of the Member States which wish to establish enhanced cooperation between themselves shall be addressed to the Council of Ministers. It shall be forwarded to the Union Minister for Foreign Affairs, who shall give an opinion on whether the enhanced cooperation is consistent with the Union's common foreign and security policy, and to the Commission, which shall give its opinion in particular on whether the enhanced cooperation proposed is consistent with other Union policies. It shall also be forwarded to the European Parliament for information.

Authorisation to proceed with enhanced cooperation shall be granted by a European decision of the Council of Ministers.

Article III-326

1.   Any Member State which wishes to participate in enhanced cooperation in one of the areas referred to in Article III-325(1) shall notify its intention to the Council of Ministers and the Commission.

The Commission shall, within four months of the date of receipt of the notification, confirm the participation of the Member State concerned. It shall note where necessary that any conditions of participation have been fulfilled and shall adopt any transitional measures deemed necessary with regard to the application of the acts already adopted within the framework of enhanced cooperation.

However, if the Commission considers that any conditions of participation have not been fulfilled, it shall indicate the arrangements to be adopted to fulfil those conditions and shall set a deadline for re-examining the request for participation. It shall re-examine the request, in accordance with the procedure set out in the preceding subparagraph. If the Commission considers that any conditions of participation have still not been met, the Member State concerned may refer the matter to the Council of Ministers, which shall act in accordance with Article I-43(3). The Council of Ministers may also adopt the transitional measures referred to in the second subparagraph on a proposal from the Commission.

2. Any Member State which wishes to participate in enhanced cooperation in the framework of the common foreign and security policy shall notify its intention to the Council of Ministers, the Union Minister for Foreign Affairs and the Commission.

The Council of Ministers shall confirm the participation of the Member State concerned, after consulting the Union Minister for Foreign Affairs. It shall note where necessary that any conditions of participation have been fulfilled. The Council of Ministers, on a proposal from the Union Minister for Foreign Affairs, may also adopt any transitional measures deemed necessary with regard to the application of the acts already adopted within the framework of enhanced cooperation. However, if the Council of Ministers considers that any conditions of participation have not been fulfilled, it shall indicate the arrangements to be adopted to fulfil those conditions and shall set a deadline for re-examining the request for participation.

For the purposes of this paragraph, the Council of Ministers shall act in accordance with Article I-43(3).

Article III-327

Expenditure resulting from implementation of enhanced cooperation, other than administrative costs entailed for the Institutions, shall be borne by the participating Member States, unless all members of the Council of Ministers, acting unanimously after consulting the European Parliament, decide otherwise.

Article III-328

Where a provision of the Constitution which may be applied in the context of enhanced cooperation stipulates that the Council of Ministers shall act unanimously, the Council of Ministers, acting unanimously in accordance with the arrangements laid down in Article I-43(3), may, on its own initiative, decide to act by qualified majority.

Where a provision of the Constitution which may be applied in the context of enhanced cooperation stipulates that the Council of Ministers shall adopt European laws or framework laws under a special legislative procedure, the Council of Ministers, acting unanimously in accordance with the arrangements laid down in Article I-43(3), may, on its own initiative, decide to act under the ordinary legislative procedure. The Council of Ministers shall act after consulting the European Parliament.

Article III-329

The Council of Ministers and the Commission shall ensure the consistency of activities undertaken in the context of enhanced cooperation and the consistency of such activities with the policies of the Union, and shall cooperate to that end.

Article III-330

Taking account of the structural economic and social situation of the French overseas departments, the Azores, Madeira and the Canary Islands, which is compounded by their remoteness, insularity, small size, difficult topography and climate, economic dependence on a few products, the permanence and combination of which severely restrain their development, the Council of Ministers, on a proposal from the Commission, shall adopt European regulations and decisions aimed, in particular, at laying down the conditions of application of the Constitution to those regions, including common policies. It shall act after consulting the European Parliament.

The measures referred to in the first paragraph concern in particular areas such as customs and trade policies, fiscal policy, free zones, agriculture and fisheries policies, conditions for supply of raw materials and essential consumer goods, State aids and conditions of access to structural funds and to horizontal Union programmes.

The Council of Ministers shall adopt the measures referred to in the first paragraph taking into account the special characteristics and constraints of the outermost regions without undermining the integrity and the coherence of the Union legal order, including the internal market and common policies.

Article III-331

The Constitution shall in no way prejudice the rules in Member States governing the system of property ownership.

Article III-332

In each of the Member States, the Union shall enjoy the most extensive legal capacity accorded to legal persons under their laws; it may, in particular, acquire or dispose of movable and immovable property and may be a party to legal proceedings. To this end, the Union shall be represented by the Commission. However, it shall be represented by each of the Institutions, by virtue of their administrative autonomy, in matters relating to their respective operation.

Article III-333

The Staff Regulations of officials and the Conditions of Employment of other servants of the Union shall be laid down by a European law. It shall be adopted after consultation of the Institutions concerned.

Article III-334

The Commission may, within the limits and under conditions laid down by a European regulation or decision adopted by a simple majority by the Council of Ministers, collect any information and carry out any checks required for the performance of the tasks entrusted to it.

Article III-335

1.　　　　　Without prejudice to Article 5 of the Protocol on the Statute of the European System of Central Banks and of the European Central Bank, measures for the production of statistics shall be laid down by a European law or framework law where necessary for the performance of the Union's activities.

2.　　　　　The production of statistics shall conform to impartiality, reliability, objectivity, scientific independence, cost-effectiveness and statistical confidentiality; it shall not entail excessive burdens on economic operators.

Article III-336

The members of the Union's Institutions, the members of committees, and the officials and other servants of the Union shall be required, even after their duties have ceased, not to disclose information of the kind covered by the obligation of professional secrecy, in particular information about undertakings, their business relations or their cost components.

Article III-337

The Union's contractual liability shall be governed by the law applicable to the contract in question.

In the case of non-contractual liability, the Union shall, in accordance with the general principles common to the laws of the Member States, make good any damage caused by its Institutions or by its servants in the performance of their duties.

The second paragraph shall apply under the same conditions to damage caused by the European Central Bank or by its servants in the performance of their duties.

The personal liability of its servants towards the Union shall be governed by the provisions laid down in their Staff Regulations or in the Conditions of Employment applicable to them.

Article III-338

The seat of the Union's Institutions shall be determined by common accord of the governments of the Member States.

Article III-339

The Council of Ministers shall adopt unanimously a European regulation laying down the rules governing the languages of the Union's Institutions, without prejudice to the Statute of the Court of Justice.

Article III-340

The Union shall enjoy in the territories of the Member States such privileges and immunities as are necessary for the performance of its tasks, under the conditions laid down in the Protocol of 8 April 1965 on the privileges and immunities of the European Communities. The same shall apply to the European Central Bank and the European Investment Bank.

Article III-341

The rights and obligations arising from agreements concluded before 1 January 1958 or, for acceding States, before the date of their accession, between one or more Member States on the one hand, and one or more third countries on the other, shall not be affected by the Constitution.

To the extent that such agreements are not compatible with the Constitution, the Member State or States concerned shall take all appropriate steps to eliminate the incompatibilities established. Member States shall, where necessary, assist each other to this end and shall, where appropriate, adopt a common attitude.

In applying the agreements referred to in the first paragraph, Member States shall take into account the fact that the advantages accorded under the Constitution by each Member State form an integral part of the Union and are thereby inseparably linked with the creation of common Institutions, the conferring of powers upon them and the granting of the same advantages by all the other Member States.

Article III-342

1.   The Constitution shall not preclude the application of the following rules:

   (a) no Member State shall be obliged to supply information the disclosure of which it considers contrary to the essential interests of its security;
   (b) any Member State may take such steps as it considers necessary for the protection of the essential interests of its security which are connected with the production of or trade in arms, munitions and war material; such steps shall not adversely affect the conditions of competition in the internal market regarding products which are not intended for specifically military purposes.

2.   The Council of Ministers, on a proposal from the Commission, may unanimously adopt a European decision making changes to the list, which it drew up on 15 April 1958, of the products to which the provisions of paragraph 1(b) apply.

PART IV

GENERAL AND FINAL PROVISIONS

Article IV-1   THE SYMBOLS OF THE UNION [1]

The flag of the Union shall be a circle of twelve golden stars on a blue background.

The anthem of the Union shall be based on the Ode to Joy from the Ninth Symphony by Ludwig van Beethoven.

The motto of the Union shall be: United in diversity.

The currency of the Union shall be the euro.

9 May shall be celebrated throughout the Union as Europe day.

Article IV-2   REPEAL OF EARLIER TREATIES

The Treaty establishing the European Community, the Treaty on European Union and the acts and treaties which have supplemented or amended them and are listed in the Protocol annexed to the Treaty establishing the Constitution shall be repealed as from the date of entry into force of the Treaty establishing the Constitution.

Article IV-3   LEGAL CONTINUITY IN RELATION TO THE EUROPEAN COMMUNITY AND THE EUROPEAN UNION

The European Union shall succeed to all the rights and obligations of the European Community and of the Union, whether internal or resulting from international agreements, which arose before the entry into force of the Treaty establishing the Constitution by virtue of previous treaties, protocols and acts, including all the assets and liabilities of the Community and of the Union, and their archives.

The provisions of the acts of the Institutions of the Union, adopted by virtue of the treaties and acts mentioned in the first paragraph, shall remain in force under the conditions laid down in the Protocol annexed to the Treaty establishing the Constitution. The case-law of the Court of Justice of the European Communities shall be maintained as a source of interpretation of Union law.

---

[1] The Convention considers that this Article would be better situated in Part I.

Article IV-4 SCOPE

1.   The Treaty establishing the Constitution shall apply to the Kingdom of Belgium, the Kingdom of Denmark, the Federal Republic of Germany, the Hellenic Republic, the Kingdom of Spain, the French Republic, Ireland, the Italian Republic, the Grand Duchy of Luxembourg, the Kingdom of the Netherlands, the Republic of Austria, the Portuguese Republic, the Republic of Finland, the Kingdom of Sweden, the United Kingdom of Great Britain and Northern Ireland, ...

2.   The Treaty establishing the Constitution shall apply to the French overseas departments, the Azores, Madeira and the Canary Islands in accordance with Article III-329 of Part III.

3.   The special arrangements for association set out in Title IV of Part III of the Treaty establishing the Constitution shall apply to the overseas countries and territories listed in Annex II to the TEC.

The Treaty establishing the Constitution shall not apply to overseas countries and territories having special relations with the United Kingdom of Great Britain and Northern Ireland which are not included in that list.

4.   The Treaty establishing the Constitution shall apply to the European territories for whose external relations a Member State is responsible.

5.   The Treaty establishing the Constitution shall apply to the Åland Islands in accordance with the provisions set out in Protocol 2 to the Act concerning the conditions of accession of the Republic of Austria, the Republic of Finland and the Kingdom of Sweden.

6.   Notwithstanding the preceding paragraphs:

(a) the Treaty establishing the Constitution shall not apply to the Faeroe Islands;

(b) the Treaty establishing the Constitution shall not apply to the sovereign base areas of the United Kingdom of Great Britain and Northern Ireland in Cyprus;

(c) the Treaty establishing the Constitution shall apply to the Channel Islands and the Isle of Man only to the extent necessary to ensure the implementation of the arrangements for those islands set out in the Treaty concerning the accession of new Member States to the European Economic Community and to the European Atomic Energy Community, signed on 22 January 1972.

Article IV-5 REGIONAL UNIONS

The Treaty establishing the Constitution shall not preclude the existence or completion of regional unions between Belgium and Luxembourg, or between Belgium, Luxembourg and the Netherlands, to the extent that the objectives of these regional unions are not attained by application of the said Treaty.

Article IV-6 PROTOCOLS

The protocols annexed to this Treaty shall form an integral part thereof.

Article IV-7 PROCEDURE FOR REVISING THE TREATY ESTABLISHING THE CONSTITUTION

1.   The government of any Member State, the European Parliament or the Commission may submit to the Council of Ministers proposals for the amendment of the Treaty establishing the Constitution. The national Parliaments of the Member States shall be notified of these proposals.

2.   If the European Council, after consulting the European Parliament and the Commission, adopts by a simple majority a decision in favour of examining the proposed amendments, the President of the European Council shall convene a Convention composed of representatives of the national Parliaments of the Member States, of the Heads of State or Government of the Member States, of the European Parliament and of the Commission. The European Central Bank shall also be consulted in the case of institutional changes in the monetary area. The European Council may decide by a simple majority, after obtaining the consent of the European Parliament, not to convene the Convention should this not be justified by the extent of the proposed amendments. In the latter case, the European Council shall define the terms of reference for the conference of representatives of the governments of the Member States.

The Convention shall examine the proposals for amendments and shall adopt by consensus a recommendation to the conference of representatives of the governments of the Member States provided for in paragraph 3.

3.   The conference of representatives of the governments of the Member States shall be convened by the President of the Council of Ministers for the purpose of determining by common accord the amendments to be made to the Treaty establishing the Constitution.

The amendments shall enter into force after being ratified by all the Member States in accordance with their respective constitutional requirements.

4.   If, two years after the signature of the treaty amending the Treaty establishing the Constitution, four fifths of the Member States have ratified it and one or more Member States have encountered difficulties in proceeding with ratification, the matter shall be referred to the European Council.

Article IV-8   ADOPTION, RATIFICATION AND ENTRY INTO FORCE OF THE TREATY ESTABLISHING THE CONSTITUTION

1.   The Treaty establishing the Constitution shall be ratified by the High Contracting Parties in accordance with their respective constitutional requirements. The instruments of ratification shall be deposited with the Government of the Italian Republic.

2.   The Treaty establishing the Constitution shall enter into force on ...., provided that all the instruments of ratification have been deposited, or, failing that, on the first day of the month following the deposit of the instrument of ratification by the last signatory State to take this step.

Article IV-9   DURATION

The Treaty establishing the Constitution is concluded for an unlimited period.

Article IV-10 LANGUAGES [2]

The Treaty establishing the Constitution, drawn up in a single original in the Danish, Dutch, English, Finnish, French, German, Greek, Irish, Italian, Portuguese, Spanish, Swedish, Czech, Estonian, Latvian, Lithuanian, Hungarian, Maltese, Polish, Slovak and Slovenian languages, the texts in each of these languages being equally authentic, shall be deposited in the archives of the Government of the Italian Republic, which will transmit a certified copy to each of the governments of the other signatory States.

---

[2] To be adjusted in accordance with the Act of Accession.

PROTOCOL
ON THE ROLE OF
NATIONAL PARLIAMENTS
IN THE EUROPEAN UNION

THE HIGH CONTRACTING PARTIES,

RECALLING that the way in which individual national Parliaments scrutinise their own governments in relation to the activities of the Union is a matter for the particular constitutional organisation and practice of each Member State,

DESIRING, however, to encourage greater involvement of national Parliaments in the activities of the European Union and to enhance their ability to express their views on legislative proposals as well as on other matters which may be of particular interest to them,

HAVE AGREED UPON the following provisions, which shall be annexed to the Constitution:

I.   INFORMATION FOR MEMBER STATES' NATIONAL PARLIAMENTS

1.   All Commission consultation documents (green and white papers and communications) shall be forwarded directly by the Commission to Member States' national Parliaments upon publication. The Commission shall also send Member States' national Parliaments the annual legislative programme as well as any other instrument of legislative planning or policy strategy that it submits to the European Parliament and to the Council of Ministers, at the same time as to those Institutions.

2.   All legislative proposals sent to the European Parliament and to the Council of Ministers shall simultaneously be sent to Member States' national Parliaments.

3.   Member States' national Parliaments may send to the Presidents of the European Parliament, the Council of Ministers and the Commission a reasoned opinion on whether a legislative proposal complies with the principle of subsidiarity, according to the procedure laid down in the Protocol on the application of the principles of subsidiarity and proportionality.

4.   A six-week period shall elapse between a legislative proposal being made available by the Commission to the European Parliament, the Council of Ministers and the Member States' national Parliaments in the official languages of the European Union and the date when it is placed on an agenda for the Council of Ministers for its adoption or for adoption of a position under a legislative procedure, subject to exceptions on grounds of urgency, the reasons for which shall be stated in the act or position of the

Council of Ministers. Save in urgent cases for which due reasons have been given, no agreement may be established on a legislative proposal during those six weeks. A ten-day period shall elapse between the placing of a proposal on the agenda for the Council of Ministers and the adoption of a position of the Council of Ministers.

5. The agendas for and the outcome of meetings of the Council of Ministers, including the minutes of meetings where the Council of Ministers is deliberating on legislative proposals, shall be transmitted directly to Member States' national Parliaments, at the same time as to Member States' governments.

6. When the European Council intends to make use of the provision of Article I-24(4), first subparagraph of the Constitution, national Parliaments shall be informed in advance.

When the European Council intends to make use of the provision of Article I-24(4), second subparagraph of the Constitution, national Parliaments shall be informed at least four months before any decision is taken.

7. The Court of Auditors shall send its annual report to Member States' national Parliaments, for information, at the same time as to the European Parliament and to the Council of Ministers.

8. In the case of bicameral national Parliaments, these provisions shall apply to both chambers.

II. INTERPARLIAMENTARY COOPERATION

9. The European Parliament and the national Parliaments shall together determine how interparliamentary cooperation may be effectively and regularly organised and promoted within the European Union.

10. The Conference of European Affairs Committees may submit any contribution it deems appropriate for the attention of the European Parliament, the Council of Ministers and the Commission. That Conference shall in addition promote the exchange of information and best practice between Member States' Parliaments and the European Parliament, including their special committees. The Conference may also organise interparliamentary conferences on specific topics, in particular to debate matters of common foreign and security policy and of common security and defence policy. Contributions from the Conference shall in no way bind national Parliaments or prejudge their positions.

PROTOCOL
ON THE APPLICATION OF THE
PRINCIPLES OF SUBSIDIARITY
AND PROPORTIONALITY

THE HIGH CONTRACTING PARTIES,

WISHING to ensure that decisions are taken as closely as possible to the citizens of the Union,

RESOLVED to establish the conditions for the application of the principles of subsidiarity and proportionality, as enshrined in Article I-9 of the Constitution, and to establish a system for monitoring the application of those principles by the Institutions,

HAVE AGREED UPON the following provisions, which shall be annexed to the Constitution:

1.   Each Institution shall ensure constant respect for the principles of subsidiarity and proportionality, as laid down in Article I-9 of the Constitution.

2.   Before proposing legislative acts, the Commission shall consult widely. Such consultations shall, where appropriate, take into account the regional and local dimension of the action envisaged. In cases of exceptional urgency, the Commission shall not conduct such consultations. It shall give reasons for the decision in its proposal.

3.   The Commission shall send all its legislative proposals and its amended proposals to the national Parliaments of the Member States at the same time as to the Union legislator. Upon adoption, legislative resolutions of the European Parliament and positions of the Council of Ministers shall be sent to the national Parliaments of the Member States.

4.   The Commission shall justify its proposal with regard to the principles of subsidiarity and proportionality. Any legislative proposal should contain a detailed statement making it possible to appraise compliance with the principles of subsidiarity and proportionality. This statement should contain some assessment of the proposal's financial impact and, in the case of a framework law, of its implications for the rules to be put in place by Member States, including, where necessary, the regional legislation. The reasons for concluding that a Union objective can be better achieved at Union level must be substantiated by qualitative and, wherever possible, quantitative indicators. The Commission shall take account of the need for any burden, whether financial or administrative, falling upon the Union, national governments, regional or local authorities, economic operators and citizens, to be minimised and commensurate with the objective to be achieved.

5.   Any national Parliament or any chamber of a national Parliament of a Member State may, within six weeks from the date of transmission of the Commission's legislative proposal, send to the Presidents of the European Parliament, the Council of Ministers and the Commission a reasoned opinion stating why it considers that the proposal in question does not comply with the principle of subsidiarity. It will be for each national Parliament or each chamber of a national Parliament to consult, where appropriate, regional parliaments with legislative powers.

6.   The European Parliament, the Council of Ministers and the Commission shall take account of the reasoned opinions issued by Member States' national Parliaments or by a chamber of a national Parliament.

The national Parliaments of Member States with unicameral Parliamentary systems shall have two votes, while each of the chambers of a bicameral Parliamentary system shall have one vote.

Where reasoned opinions on a Commission proposal's non-compliance with the principle of subsidiarity represent at least one third of all the votes allocated to the Member States' national Parliaments and their chambers, the Commission shall review its proposal. This threshold shall be at least a quarter in the case of a Commission proposal or an initiative emanating from a group of Member States under the provisions of Article III-165 of the Constitution on the area of freedom, security and justice.

After such review, the Commission may decide to maintain, amend or withdraw its proposal. The Commission shall give reasons for its decision.

7.   The Court of Justice shall have jurisdiction to hear actions on grounds of infringement of the principle of subsidiarity by a legislative act, brought in accordance with the rules laid down in Article III-270 of the Constitution by Member States, or notified by them in accordance with their legal order on behalf of their national Parliament or a chamber of it.

In accordance with the same Article of the Constitution, the Committee of the Regions may also bring such actions as regards legislative acts for the adoption of which the Constitution provides that it be consulted.

8.　　　　　The Commission shall submit each year to the European Council, the European Parliament, the Council of Ministers and the national Parliaments of the Member States a report on the application of Article I-9 of the Constitution. This annual report shall also be forwarded to the Committee of the Regions and to the Economic and Social Committee.

PROTOCOL ON THE REPRESENTATION OF CITIZENS IN THE EUROPEAN PARLIAMENT AND THE WEIGHTING OF VOTES IN THE EUROPEAN COUNCIL AND THE COUNCIL OF MINISTERS

THE HIGH CONTRACTING PARTIES,

HAVE ADOPTED the following provisions, which shall be annexed to the Treaty establishing a Constitution for Europe:

Article 1: PROVISIONS CONCERNING THE EUROPEAN PARLIAMENT

1. Throughout the 2004-2009 parliamentary term, the number of representatives elected to the European Parliament in each Member State shall be as follows:

Belgium	24
Czech Republic	24
Denmark	14
Germany	99
Estonia	6
Greece	24
Spain	54
France	78
Ireland	13
Italy	78
Cyprus	6
Latvia	9
Lithuania	13
Luxembourg	6
Hungary	24
Malta	5
Netherlands	27
Austria	18
Poland	54
Portugal	24
Slovenia	7
Slovakia	14
Finland	14
Sweden	19
United Kingdom	78

Article 2   PROVISIONS CONCERNING THE WEIGHTING OF VOTES IN THE EUROPEAN COUNCIL AND THE COUNCIL OF MINISTERS

1.   The following provisions shall remain in force until 1 November 2009, without prejudice to Article I-24 of the Constitution.

For deliberations of the European Council and of the Council of Ministers requiring a qualified majority, members' votes shall be weighted as follows:

Belgium	12
Czech Republic	12
Denmark	7
Germany	29
Estonia	4
Greece	12
Spain	27
France	29
Ireland	7
Italy	29
Cyprus	4
Latvia	4
Lithuania	7
Luxembourg	4
Hungary	12
Malta	3
Netherlands	13
Austria	10
Poland	27
Portugal	12
Slovenia	4
Slovakia	7
Finland	7
Sweden	10
United Kingdom	29

Decisions shall be adopted if there are at least 232 votes in favour representing a majority of the members where, under the Constitution, they must be adopted on a proposal from the Commission. In other cases decisions shall be adopted if there are at least 232 votes in favour representing at least two thirds of the members.

A member of the European Council or the Council of Ministers may request that, where a decision is taken by the European Council or the Council of Ministers by a qualified majority, a check is made to ensure that the Member States comprising the qualified majority represent at least 62% of the total population of the Union. If that proves not to be the case, the decision shall not be adopted.

2.   For subsequent accessions, the threshold referred to in paragraph 1 shall be calculated to ensure that the qualified majority threshold expressed in votes does not exceed that resulting from the table in the Declaration on the enlargement of the European Union in the Final Act of the Conference which adopted the Treaty of Nice.

PROTOCOL
ON THE EURO GROUP

THE HIGH CONTRACTING PARTIES,

Desiring to promote conditions for stronger economic growth in Europe and, to that end, to develop ever-closer coordination of economic policies within the euro area,

Conscious of the need to lay down special provisions for enhanced dialogue between the Member States which have adopted the euro, pending the accession of all Member States of the Union to the euro area,

Have agreed upon the following provisions, which are annexed to the Constitution:

Article 1

The Ministers of the Member States which have adopted the euro shall meet informally. Such meetings shall take place, when necessary, to discuss questions related to the specific responsibilities they share with regard to the single currency. The Commission and the European Central Bank shall be invited to take part in such meetings, which shall be prepared by the representatives of the Ministers with responsibility for finance of the Member States which have adopted the euro.

Article 2

The Ministers of the Member States which have adopted the euro shall elect a president for two and a half years, by a majority of those Member States.

PROTOCOL
AMENDING THE EURATOM TREATY

THE HIGH CONTRACTING PARTIES,

RECALLING the necessity that the provisions of the Treaty establishing the European Atomic Energy Community should continue to have full legal effect,

DESIROUS however to adapt that Treaty to the new rules established by the Treaty establishing a Constitution for Europe, in particular in the institutional and financial fields,

HAVE ADOPTED the following provisions, which are annexed to the Treaty establishing a Constitution for Europe and amend the Treaty establishing the European Atomic Energy Community as follows:

Article 1

Article 3 shall be repealed.

Article 2

The heading of Title III "Institutional provisions" shall be replaced by the following: "Institutional and financial provisions".

Article 3

1.   Article 107 shall be replaced by the following:

"Article 107

The institutional and financial provisions of the Treaty establishing a Constitution for Europe (Articles I-18 to I-38, Articles I-52 to I-55 and Articles III-227 to III-316) and Article I-58 of that Treaty shall apply to this Treaty without prejudice to the specific provisions laid down in Articles 134, 135, 144, 145, 157, 171, 172, 174 and 176.

2.   Articles 107a to 133, 136 to 143, 146 to 156, 158 to 170, 173, 173a, 175, and 177 to 183a shall be repealed."

Article 4

The heading of Title IV "Financial provisions" shall be replaced by the following:

"Specific financial provisions".

Article 5

In the third paragraph of Article 38 and the third paragraph of Article 82 the references to Articles 141 and 142 shall be replaced by references to Articles III-265 and III-266 respectively of the Treaty establishing a Constitution for Europe.

In Article 171(2), the first paragraph of Article 175, and Article 176(3) the references to Article 183 shall be replaced by references to Article III-318 of the Treaty establishing a Constitution for Europe.

In Article 172(4) the reference to Article 177(5) shall be replaced by a reference to Article III-310 of the Treaty establishing a Constitution for Europe.

In the last paragraph of Article 18 and in Article 83(2) the references to Article 164 shall be replaced by references to Article III-307 of the Treaty establishing a Constitution for Europe.

In Articles 38 and 82 the word "directive" shall be replaced by "European decision".

In the Treaty the word "decision" shall be replaced by "European decision".

Article 6

Article 190 shall be replaced by the following:

"The rules governing the languages of the Institutions shall, without prejudice to the provisions contained in the Statute of the Court of Justice, be determined by the Council of Ministers, acting unanimously".

Article 7

Article 198 shall be amended as follows:

"(a) This Treaty shall not apply to the Faeroe Islands".

Article 8

Article 201 shall be amended as follows:

"The Community shall establish close cooperation with the Organisation for Economic Cooperation and Development, the details of which shall be determined by common accord".

Article 9

Article 206 shall be amended as follows:

"The Community may conclude with one or more States or international organisations agreements establishing an association involving reciprocal rights and obligations, common action and special procedures.

These agreements shall be concluded by the Council of Ministers, acting unanimously after consulting the European Parliament.

Where such agreements call for amendments to this Treaty, these amendments shall first be adopted in accordance with the procedure laid down in Article IV-7 of the Treaty establishing a Constitution for Europe.".

DECLARATION
ATTACHED TO THE PROTOCOL
ON THE REPRESENTATION OF CITIZENS
IN THE EUROPEAN PARLIAMENT AND
THE WEIGHTING OF VOTES IN THE
EUROPEAN COUNCIL AND
THE COUNCIL OF MINISTERS

The common position which will be taken by the Member States of the European Union at the conferences on the accession of Romania and/or Bulgaria regarding the allocation of seats in the European Parliament and the weighting of votes in the European Council and the Council of Ministers shall be as follows. If the accession to the European Union of Romania and/or Bulgaria takes place before the entry into force of the European Council decision foreseen in Article I-19(2) of the Constitution, the number of their elected representatives to the European Parliament shall be calculated on the basis of the figures of 33 and 17 respectively, corrected according to the same formula as that which determined the number of representatives in the European Parliament for each Member State as indicated in the Protocol on the representation of citizens in the European Parliament and the weighting of votes in the European Council and the Council of Ministers.

The Treaty of Accession to the European Union may, by way of derogation from Article I-19(2) of the Constitution, stipulate that the number of members of the European Parliament may temporarily exceed 736 for the remainder of the 2004 to 2009 Parliamentary term.

Without prejudice to Article I-24(2) of the Constitution, the weighting of the votes of Romania and Bulgaria in the European Council and the Council of Ministers shall be 14 and 10 respectively until 1 November 2009. At the time of each accession, the threshold referred to in the Protocol on the representation of citizens in the European Parliament and the weighting of votes in the European Council and the Council of Ministers shall be decided by the Council of Ministers.

DECLARATION
ON THE CREATION
OF A EUROPEAN EXTERNAL
ACTION SERVICE

"To assist the future Union Minister for Foreign Affairs, introduced in Article I-27 of the Constitution, to perform his or her duties, the Convention agrees on the need for the Council of Ministers and the Commission to agree, without prejudice to the rights of the European Parliament, to establish under the Minister's authority one joint service (European External Action Service) composed of officials from relevant departments of the General Secretariat of the Council of Ministers and of the Commission and staff seconded from national diplomatic services.

The staff of the Union's delegations, as defined in Article III-230, shall be provided from this joint service.

The Convention is of the view that the necessary arrangements for the establishment of the joint service should be made within the first year after entry into force of the Treaty establishing a Constitution for Europe."

DECLARATION
IN THE FINAL
ACT OF SIGNATURE OF THE TREATY
ESTABLISHING THE CONSTITUTION

If, two years after the signature of the Treaty establishing the Constitution, four fifths of the Member States have ratified it and one or more Member States have encountered difficulties in proceeding with ratification, the matter will be referred to the European Council.

THE EUROPEAN CONVENTION
LIST OF MEMBERS

PRESIDENCY

Mr Valéry Giscard d'Estaing
Chairman

Mr Giuliano Amato
Vice-Chairman

Mr Jean-Luc Dehaene
Vice-Chairman

OTHER MEMBERS
OF THE PRAESIDIUM

Mr Michel Barnier
Representative of the European Commission

Mr John Bruton
Representative of the National Parliaments

Mr Henning Christophersen
Representative of the Danish Presidency

Mr Alfonso Dastis
Representative of the Spanish Presidency
(from March 2003)

Mr Klaus Hänsch
Representative of the European Parliament

Mr Giorgos Katiforis
Representative of the Greek Presidency
(until February 2003)

Mr Iñigo Méndez De Vigo y Montojo
Representative of the European Parliament

Ms Ana Palacio
Representative of the Spanish Presidency
(until March 2003)

Mr Giorgos Papandreou
Representative of the Greek Presidency
(from February 2003)

Ms Giscla Stuart
Representative of the National Parliaments

Mr Antonio Vitorino
Representative of the European Commission

Mr Alojz Peterle
Invitee

CONVENTION MEMBERS

REPRESENTATIVES
OF THE EUROPEAN PARLIAMENT

Mr Jens-Peter Bonde (DK)

Mr Elmar Brok (D)

Mr Andrew Nicholas Duff (UK)

Mr Olivier Duhamel (F)

Mr Klaus Hänsch (D)

Ms Sylvia-Yvonne Kaufmann (D)

Mr Timothy Kirkhope (UK)

Mr Alain Lamassoure (F)

Ms Linda McAvan (UK)

Ms Hanja Maij-Weggen (NL)

Mr Luís Marinho (P)

Mr Íñigo Méndez De Vigo y Montojo (ES)

Ms Cristiana Muscardini (IT)

Mr Antonio Tajani (IT)

Ms Anne Van Lancker (B)

Mr Johannes Voggenhuber (ÖS)

REPRESENTATIVES
OF THE COMMISSION

Mr Michel Barnier

Mr António Vitorino

REPRESENTATIVES
OF THE MEMBER STATES

BELGIË/BELGIQUE

Government

Mr Louis Michel

National Parliament

Mr Karel de Gucht

Mr Elio di Rupo

DANMARK

Government
Mr Henning Christophersen

National Parliament
Mr Peter Skaarup
Mr Henrik Dam Kristensen

DEUTSCHLAND

Government
Mr Joschka Fischer
replaced Mr Peter Glotz in November 2002

National Parliament
Mr Jürgen Meyer
Mr Erwin Teufel

ELLAS

Government
Mr Giorgos Papandreou
replaced Mr Giorgos KATIFORIS in February 2003

National Parliament
Mr Paraskevas Avgerinos
Ms Marietta Giannakou

ESPAÑA

Government
Mr Alfonso Dastis
replaced Mr Carlos Bastarreche as alternate member
in September 2002, then Ms A. Palacio as member
in March 2003

National Parliament
Mr Josep Borrell Fontelles
Mr Gabriel Cisneros Laborda

FRANCE

Government
Mr Dominique de Villepin
replaced Mr Pierre Moscovici
in November 2002

National Parliament
Mr Pierre Lequiller
replaced Mr Alain Barrau in July 2002
Mr Hubert Haenel

IRELAND

Government
Mr Dick Roche
replaced Mr Ray MacSharry in July 2002

National Parliament
Mr John Bruton
Mr Proinsias de Rossa

ITALIA

Government
Mr Gianfranco Fini

National Parliament
Mr Marco Follini
Mr Lamberto Dini

LUXEMBOURG

Government
Mr Jacques Santer

National Parliament
Mr Paul Helminger
Mr Ben Fayot

NEDERLAND

Government
Mr Gijs de Vries
replaced Mr Hans van Mierlo in October 2002

National Parliament
Mr René van der Linden
Mr Frans Timmermans

ÖSTERREICH

Government
Mr Hannes Farnleitner

National Parliament
Mr Caspar Einem
Mr Reinhard Eugen Bösch

PORTUGAL

Government
Mr Ernâni Lopes
replaced Mr João de Vallera in May 2002

National Parliament
Mr Alberto Costa
Ms Eduarda Azevedo

SUOMI/FINLAND

Government
Ms Teija Tiilikainen

National Parliament
Mr Kimmo Kiljunen
Mr Jari Vilén
replaced Mr Matti Vanhanen
in May 2003

SVERIGE

Government
Ms Lena Hjelm-Wallén

National Parliament
Mr Sören Lekberg
Mr Göran Lennmarker

UNITED KINGDOM

Government
Mr Peter Hain

National Parliament
Ms Gisela Stuart
Mr David Heathcoat-Amory

REPRESENTATIVES
OF THE CANDIDATE COUNTRIES

ΚΥΠΡΟΣ/CYPRUS

Government
Mr Michael Attalides

National Parliament
Ms Eleni Mavrou
Mr Panayiotis Demetriou

MALTA

Government
Mr Peter Serracino-Inglott

National Parliament
Mr Michael Frendo
Mr Alfred Sant

MAGYARORSZÀG/HUNGARY

Government
Mr Péter Balázs
replaced Mr János Martonyi in June 2002

National Parliament
Mr József Szájer
Mr Pál Vastagh

POLSKA/POLAND

Government
Ms Danuta Hübner

National Parliament
Mr Jozef Oleksy
Mr Edmund Wittbrodt

ROMÂNIA/ROMANIA

Government
Ms Hildegard Carola Puwak

National Parliament
Mr Alexandru Athanasiu
replaced Mr Liviu Maior in February 2003
Mr Puiu Hasotti

SLOVENSKO/SLOVAKIA

Government
Mr Ivan Korčok
replaced Mr Ján Figel in November 2002

National Parliament
Mr Ján Figel
replaced Mr Pavol Hamzik in October 2002
Ms Irena Belohorská

LATVIJA/LATVIA

Government
Ms Sandra Kalniete
replaced Mr Roberts Zile in January 2003

National Parliament
Mr Rihards Piks
Ms Liene Liepina
replaced Mr Edvins Inkēns in January 2003

EESTI/ESTONIA

Government
Mr Lennart Meri

National Parliament
Mr Tunne Kelam
Mr Rein Lang
replaced Mr Peeter Reitzberg in April 2003

LIETUVA/LITHUANIA

Government
Mr Rytis Martikonis

National Parliament
Mr Vytenis Andriukaitis
Mr Algirdas Gricius
in December 2002 replaced Mr Alvydas
Medalinskas, who in turn replaced
Ms Dalia Kutraite-Giedraitiene as alternate
member

БЪЛГАРИЯ/BULGARIA

Government
Ms Meglena Kuneva

National Parliament
Mr Daniel Valchev
Mr Nikolai Mladenov

ČESKÁ REPUBLIKA/CZECH REPUBLIC

Government
Mr Jan Kohout
replaced Mr Jan Kavan
in September 2002

National Parliament
Mr Jan Zahradil
Mr Josef Zieleniec

SLOVENIJA/SLOVENIA

Government
Mr Dimitrij Rupel
replaced Mr Matjaz Nahtigal
in January 2003

National Parliament
Mr Jelko Kacin
replaced Mr Slavko Gaber
in January 2003

Mr Alojz Peterle

TÜRQÍYE/TURKEY

Government
Mr Abdullah Gül
in March 2003 replaced
Mr Yasar Yakis, who had replaced Mr Mesut Yilmaz
in December 2002

National Parliament
Mr Zekeriya Akcam
replaced Mr Ali Tekin
in December 2002

Mr Kemal Derviş
replaced Ms Ayfer Yilmaz in December 2002

ALTERNATES

REPRESENTATIVES
OF THE EUROPEAN PARLIAMENT

Mr William Abitbol (F)

Ms Almeida Garrett (P)

Mr John Cushnahan (IRL)

Ms Lone Dybkjaer (DK)

Ms Pervenche Berès (F)

Ms Maria Berger (ÖS)

Mr Carlos Carnero González (ES)

Mr Neil MacCormick (UK)

Ms Piia-Noora Kauppi (FI)

Ms Elena Paciotti (IT)

Mr Luís Queiró (P)

Mr Reinhard Rack (ÖS)

Mr Esko Seppänen (FI)

The Earl of Stockton (UK)

Ms Helle Thorning-Schmidt (DK)

Mr Joachim Wuermeling (D)

REPRESENTATIVES
OF THE COMMISSION

Mr David O'Sullivan

Mr Paolo Ponzano

REPRESENTATIVES
OF THE MEMBER STATES

BELGIË/BELGIQUE

Government

Mr Pierre Chevalier

National Parliament

Mr Danny Pieters

Ms Marie Nagy

DANMARK

Government
Mr Poul Schlüter

National Parliament
Mr Per Dalgaard
Mr Niels Helveg Petersen

DEUTSCHLAND

Government
Mr Hans Martin Bury
replaced Mr Gunter Pleuger
in November 2002

National Parliament
Mr Peter Altmaier
Mr Wolfgang Gerhards
replaced Mr Wolfgang Senff in March 2003

ELLAS

Government
Mr Giorgos Katiforis
replaced Mr Panayiotis Ioakimidis in February 2003

National Parliament
Mr Nikolaos Constantopoulos
Mr Evripidis Stiliniadis

ESPAÑA

Government
Ms Ana Palacio
replaced Mr Alfonso Dastis in March 2003

National Parliament
Mr Diego López Garrido
Mr Alejandro Muñoz Lonso

FRANCE

Government
Ms Pascale Andreani
replaced Mr Pierre Vimont
in August 2002

National Parliament
Mr Jacques Floch
replaced Ms Anne-Marie Idrac
in July 2002
Mr Robert Badinter

IRELAND

Government
Mr Bobby McDonagh

National Parliament
Mr Pat Carey,
replaced Mr Martin Cullen in July 2002
Mr John Gormley

ITALIA

Government
Mr Francesco E. Speroni

National Parliament
Mr Valdo Spini
Mr Filadelfio Guido Basile

LUXEMBOURG

Government
Mr Nicolas Schmit

National Parliament
Mr Gaston Giberyen
Ms Renée Wagener

NEDERLAND

Government
Mr Thom de Bruijn

National Parliament
Mr Wim van Eekelen
Mr Jan Jacob van Dijk
replaced Mr Hans van Baalen in October 2002

ÖSTERREICH

Government
Mr Gerhard Tusek

National Parliament
Ms Evelin Lichtenberger
Mr Eduard Mainoni
replaced Mr Gerhard Kurzmann
in March 2003

PORTUGAL

Government
Mr Manuel Lobo Antunes

National Parliament
Mr Guilherme d'Oliveira Martins
replaced Mr Osvaldo de Castro
in June 2002
Mr António Nazaré Pereira

SUOMI/FINLAND

Government
Mr Antti Peltomäki

National Parliament
Mr Hannu Takkula
replaced Ms Riitta Korhonen
in May 2003
Mr Esko Helle

SVERIGE

Government
Mr Sven-Olof Petersson
replaced Ms Lena Hallengren
in December 2002

National Parliament
Mr Kenneth Kvist
Mr Ingvar Svensson

UNITED KINGDOM

Government
Baroness Scotland of Asthal

National Parliament
Lord Tomlinson
Lord Maclennan of Rogart

REPRESENTATIVES
OF THE CANDIDATE COUNTRIES

ΚΥΠΡΟΣ/CYPRUS

Government
Mr Theophilos V. Theophilou

National Parliament
Mr Marios Matsakis
Ms Androula Vassiliou

MALTA

Government
Mr John Inguanez

National Parliament
Ms Dolores Cristina
Mr George Vella

MAGYARORSZÀG/HUNGARY

Government
Mr Péter Gottfried

National Parliament
Mr András Kelemen
Mr István Szent-Iványi

POLSKA/POLAND

Government
Mr Janusz Trzciński

National Parliament
Ms Marta Fogler
Ms Genowefa Grabowska

ROMÂNIA/ROMANIA

Government
Mr Constantin Ene
replaced Mr Ion Jinga in December 2002

National Parliament
Mr Péter Eckstein-Kovacs
Mr Adrian Severin

SLOVENSKO/SLOVAKIA

Government
Mr Juraj Migaš

National Parliament
Ms Zuzana Martinakova
replaced Mr Frantisek Sebej
in November 2002
Mr Boris Zala
replaced Ms Olga Keltosova
in November 2002

LATVIJA/LATVIA

Government
Mr Roberts Zile
replaced Mr Guntars Krasts in January 2003

National Parliament
Mr Guntars Krasts
replaced Mr Maris Sprindzuks
in January 2003
Mr Arturs Krisjanis Karins
replaced Ms Inese Birzniece
in January 2003

EESTI/ESTONIA

Government
Mr Henrik Hololei

National Parliament
Ms Liina Tõnisson
replaced Ms Liia Hänni in April 2003
Mr Urmas Reinsalu
replaced Mr Ülo Tärno in April 2003

LIETUVA/LITHUANIA

Government
Mr Oskaras Jusys

National Parliament
Mr Gintautas Šivickas
in February 2003 replaced
Mr Gediminas Dalinkevicius,
who had replaced Mr Rolandas Pavilionis in
December 2002
Mr Eugenijus Maldeikis
replaced Mr Alvydas Medalinskas in
February 2003

БЪЛГАРИЯ/BULGARIA

Government
Ms Neli Kutskova

National Parliament
Mr Alexander Arabadjiev
Mr Nesrin Uzun

ČESKÁ REPUBLIKA/CZECH REPUBLIC

Government
Ms Lenka Anna Rovna
replaced Mr Jan Kohout
 in September 2002

National Parliament
Mr Petr Nečas
Mr František Kroupa

SLOVENIJA/SLOVENIA

Government
Mr Janez Lenarčič

National Parliament
Mr Franc Horvat
replaced Ms Danica Simšič
in January 2003
Mr Mihael Brejc

TÜRQÍYE/TURKEY

Government
Mr Oğuz Demiralp
replaced Mr Nihat Akyol
in August 2002

National Parliament
Mr Ibrahim Özal
replaced Mr Kürsat Eser
in December 2002
Mr Necdet Budak
replaced Mr A. Emre Kocaoglou
in December 2002

OBSERVERS

Mr Roger Briesch
Economic and Social Committee

Mr Josef Chabert
Committee of the Regions

Mr João Cravinho
European Social Partners

Mr Manfred Dammeyer
Committee of the Regions

Mr Patrick Dewael
Committee of the Regions

Mr Nikiforos Diamandouros
European Ombudsman (replaced Mr Jacob Söderman
in March 2003)

Ms Claude du Granrut
Committee of the Regions

Mr Göke Daniel Frerichs
Economic and Social Committee

Mr Emilio Gabaglio
European Social Partners

Mr Georges Jacobs
European Social Partners

Mr Claudio Martini
Committee of the Regions

Ms Anne-Maria Sigmund
Economic and Social Committee

Mr Ramón Luis Valcárcel Siso
Committee of the Regions (replaced
Mr Eduardo Zaplana in February 2003;
Ms Eva-Riitta Siitonen had acted as alternate since
October 2002)

SECRETARIAT

Sir John Kerr
Secretary-General

Ms Annalisa Giannella
Deputy Secretary-General

Ms Marta Arpio Santacruz

Ms Agnieszka Bartol

Mr Hervé Bribosia

Ms Nicole Buchet

Ms Elisabeth Gateau

Mr Clemens Ladenburger

Ms Maria José Martínez Iglesias

Mr Nikolaus Meyer Landrut

Mr Guy Milton

Mr Ricardo Passos

Ms Kristin de Peyron

Mr Alain Pilette

Mr Alain Piotrowski

Mr Etienne de Poncins

Ms Alessandra Schiavo

Ms Walpurga Speckbacher

Ms Maryem van den Heuvel

TABLE OF CONTENTS

PART II
THE CHARTER OF FUNDAMENTAL RIGHTS OF THE UNION   55

European Convention

Draft treaty establishing a Constitution for Europe
Adopted by consensus by the European Convention on 13 June and 10 July 2003
Submitted to the President of the European Council in Rome — 18 July 2003

Luxembourg: Office for Official Publications of the European Communities

2003 — VIII – 333 pp. — 17.6 x 25 cm

ISBN 92-78-40197-8